The Colour of the Skunk

A Policeman's Diary in Apartheid South Africa

Wilson Lwandhle Magadhla

Copyright © 2022 Wilson Lwandhle Magadhla.

All rights reserved.

This publication may not be reproduced, in whole or in part, by any means including photocopying or using any information storage or retrieval system, without specific and prior written permission of the publisher.

This book is sold subject to the condition that it shall not, by way of trade or otherwise, be re-sold, hired out, or otherwise circulated without the publisher's prior consent in any form of binding or cover other than that in which it is published and without a similar condition including this condition being imposed on the subsequent purchaser.

First Edition: February 2022

Published by: Nsemia Inc. Publishers
www.nsemia.com

Edited: Estella Muyinda
Cover Concept & Illustration: Kemunto Nyanyuki
Cover Design: Linda Kiboma
Layout Design: Bethsheba Nyabuto

Note for Librarians:
A cataloguing record for this book is available from Library and Archives Canada.

ISBN: 978-1-989928-21-9

Table of Contents

Dedication v
A Word from the Publisher...vi
Acknowledgements vii
Prologue ix
Introduction xi

PART 1: ENTRY INTO THE POLICE FORCE XIII

   Chapter 1: The Journey Begins 1
   Chapter 2: My Recruitment 3
   Chapter 3: From the Durban Station to the Bluff................... 7
   Chapter 4: The Security Branch Interview 9
   Chapter 5: Police Training 11
   Chapter 6: Starting as a Constable Recruit........................... 17
   Chapter 7: The Cato Manor Riots 19
   Chapter 8: The Paranoid Sergeant 29
   Chapter 9: The Scare of my Life.. 31
   Chapter 10: Association with a Liberal Party Family 33

PART 2: COLOUR, FAITH AND RANK................................. 37

   Chapter 11: The Security Branch 39
   Chapter 12: The Homelands 45
   Chapter 13: A Letter to Prince Buthelezi 47
   Chapter 14: Joining the Detectives 51
   Chapter 15: Making my First Impact at a New Station 57
   Chapter 16: Poor, yet Arrogant and Demeaning 61
   Chapter 17: The Day I Saw Apartheid Kill a White Man 63
   Chapter 18: A Young White Police Detective's First Kill 67
   Chapter 19: A No-Win Situation 69
   Chapter 20: We were an Invisible Team 73
   Chapter 21: The Two Twits' Dilemma................................... 77
   Chapter 22: Black Policemen Helping White Racists 81
   Chapter 23: The Laundry Thief.. 85

PART 3: SKILL & HONOUR ... 89
Chapter 24: How I Earned Trust from Criminals ... 91
Chapter 25: Respect and Recognition ... 97
PART 4: Intrigues and Woes ... 99
Chapter 26: UDF & IFP Wars in Pietermaritzburg ... 101
Chapter 27: The Third Force ... 105
Chapter 28: Five Bodies Under the Paradise Bridge ... 109
Chapter 29: Interference by Senior Officers ... 113
Chapter 30: Kwa Ndebele the Stinking Skunk in its True Colours ... 119
PART 4: PROFESSIONALISM, GOOD HEARTS & APARTHEID 135
Chapter 31: I need some answers ... 137
Chapter 32: My Tool to Tilt the Granite Wall ... 145
Chapter 33: Sergeant Bartels ... 147
Chapter 34: Captain Dutton and I ... 149
PART 5: DESPAIR VERSUS HOPE ... 155
Chapter 35: Candles of Hope ... 157
Chapter 36: Waving the Red Flag in Front of a Spanish Bull 171
Chapter 37: Ten O'clock Tea at Police Quarters ... 173
Chapter 38: On the System & its View of Me ... 177
Chapter 39: The Final Curtain ... 181
EPILOGUE ... 185
PICTORIALS ... 188

Dedication

I dedicate this book to my loving mother, the late Nomnyaka Salomi Magadhla.

A Word from the Publisher

South Africa has been of interest to me since the days of my youth. The racist regime and its audacious implementation usually generated sad and memorable headlines in major news outlets across the world such as the BBC, Radio Deutsche Welle and Voice of America. It featured a lot in the foreign news section of the Voice of Kenya, now called the Kenya Broadcasting Corporation. This was because of the internal conflict that arose within South Africa and incursions the country's forces made into what came to be referred to as "the frontline states"; countries that were at the forefront of the liberation of Africa and suffered the brunt of their actions. With time, Nelson Mandela became the most famous and celebrated political prisoner of the time; a household name.

I met the late Lwandhle Magadhla in 2009 through S'bu Xulu, an ANC insider, who had some work with the Government of KwaZulu-Natal which a team of us were helping with. On learning that we published books, S'bu quickly connected me with the author.

Meeting with and talking to Mr. Magadhla, as he narrated about his time in the apartheid police force, was awe-inspiring. Discovering that he had chronicled this thought-provoking experience, in very succinct ways, made it even more interesting. It is a story we could not ignore and one we committed to publish.

Unfortunately, as fate would have it, Mr. Magadhla was called by The Maker as we worked on his manuscripts, one of which was published under the title *Philosophical Escapades*, ISBN 978-1926906126 (Nsemia Inc. 2012). We had an obligation to publish this work, both contractually and for its value and we have made good that commitment.

I hope that this work better illuminates the chapter of history of South Africa that it covers. Further, I hope that it offers lessons from the character and professionalism of a fine man who worked to excel in difficult circumstances but also found the devilish and humane sides of people regardless of their skin colour.

Matunda Nyanchama
Publisher

Acknowledgements

I shall forever relish the honour accorded to me by former Judge President of the Constitutional Court, Justice Pius Langa, when he acceded to my request for legal advice on certain aspects of this book. The empowerment and encouragement gained, strengthened my resolve to see this book in print. I am also indebted to Judge Justice Poswa for valuable advice regarding the legal aspects of this book, which he enthusiastically gave when I sought his opinion.

I'm grateful to Dr. Matunda Nyanchama for his warmth and enthusiasm in encouraging me in my effort to get this book and other material I have authored to the publishing table. Besides providing me with the necessary advice, he saw to it that I got two lady typists, Ms. Samukelisiwe Madlala and Nonkuleko Ndlela, both of whom provided commendable professional services. Mr. Cyril Madlala (former editor of UmAfrica) for his time in helping me with typing and advice when I was in dire need.

My special tribute goes to my son Vuyisile, with whom I saw the book to completion. My daughter Zimbili played an important role in administrative matters regarding liaison with the publishing company. My son Mangi offered advice in contractual and academic matters. Last, but not least, my family offered understanding even when the demands placed upon me in seeing this book through deprived them of my attention.

Prologue

I have toyed with the idea of writing this book for many years. There have been so many conferences and debates in my mind about why and how my story as a black policeman in the South African Police Force, during the apartheid era, should be told. Whether it should be told at all, and by me, I felt it was absolutely necessary. As to how it should be told became clearly another matter requiring a lot of soul searching. There had to be a careful weighing of some of the material to be involved. The issues included the question of the lapse of time in relation to the post-apartheid era and the present, the reconciliatory spirit the new democratic South Africa seeks to achieve, mentioning names of individuals and the legal implications thereof.

One thing I realized was that my story 'did not want' to remain untold and unknown. Though at times I have been tempted to keep it that way, it has refused to remain untold. It claims that it has a right to be told and to be known. I, not given to denying rights to any one, succumbed to the urge to tell the story. As a consequence, I have embarked on this gruelling journey of pen and paper for which I pray for your supportive company.

There have been many a feeding frenzy by journalists, researchers and analysts into what characterized members of the South African Police under the apartheid government. According to the perspective of the general white public, black policemen were almost non-existent. They were, as if hidden in the backyard, without names or faces. Their names and faces were never seen on television or mentioned in newspapers as having achieved anything of importance.

In the eyes of South African black communities, they depicted themselves as hard and merciless in carrying out the implementation of the much hated apartheid policy of passbook check-ups with sometimes extraordinary enthusiasm, accompanied by complete disrespect and disregard of the age, gender and personal circumstances of the people they searched and violated. It was as if the black policemen involved were ignorant and did not mind the fact that the pass laws and the Group Areas Act were meant to effectively control the lives of their own people. It was as if they felt exempt from the harsh realities and the cold effects of the dreadful apartheid laws. The fact is that, once they were recruited and took oath of loyalty, they were like any member of the South African Police Force, and were expected to carry out their duties according to the law. One of them was to demand pass books and arrest those who did not have the documents in their possession or did not have documents at all for reasons beyond their control.

Every black policeman, with any semblance of pride and honour, carried out such duties with a pinch of pain and guilt and would, at times, give pass offenders a chance when he was not within sight of white colleagues and those black members regarded as blind loyalists. Of course every policeman under normal circumstances was supposed to be loyal to the South African Police Force and the government of the day, but as apartheid itself was far from being a normal government, normal circumstances were not part of the equation. Personal discretion, when circumstances, allowed was the best way out for those whose conscience dictated against blind loyalty to apartheid.

Although there were a host of highly objectionable and vexatious apartheid laws, fortunately for all citizens, no policeman was barred from dealing with common law crimes. There was, however, some measure of interference where certain investigations threatened the comfort of those apartheid police bosses who had rated the interests of apartheid higher than those of the general public.

In line with the policy of apartheid, black policemen were not supposed to carry dockets where white people were complainants or suspects.

There was room for those black policemen who were dedicated to the suppression and control of crime as it affected innocent and unsuspecting victims among all South Africans and indeed there was appreciation for such efforts by such policemen from the law courts, the victims and the general public.

Dedicated, impartial and honest policemen contributed in the great effort to save the country by exposing, at great risk to their own lives, elements within the security forces who had opted for the elimination of all those who sympathized, advocated and campaigned for the end of apartheid and the attainment of a truly democratic South Africa.

At this point, my message to the reader is: brace yourself for a guaranteed blow-by-blow and step-by-step account of an amazing journey by a black policeman through the turmoil, the anguish and the agony in the mayhem and madness of apartheid South Africa.

Wilson Lwandhle Magadhla

Introduction

Some people feel that it is time that the apartheid story were laid to rest. They say that it has been milked dry and done to death. I say they are wrong. Apartheid was about racism, institutionalized racism. It was about power in the hands of the wrong people, shameless greed, hatred and arrogance. There can be no time line or limit to the effort, by peace lovers o the world over, for input toward a cure to the cancerous disease of racism.

The entire apartheid ideology was simply sugar-coated racism. One would have to be extremely gullible and naïve or be an inhabitant of another world to be completely unaffected by racism. It is very sad that the advocates and the disciples of racism, be it from any quarter of the village of human kind, exist under an affliction of a fog of forgetfulness. It seems as if they will never learn. There were many opportunities from which they could learn and change their inappropriate behaviours.

There is hardly a library in the civilized world whose shelves are not adorned with books about apartheid. Scholars and analysts have delved into and dissected the apartheid animal with glee and purpose so that, by now, they comfortably rest, thinking that their quest for knowledge has been achieved and their thirst for answers quenched. But this is apartheid I am talking about. I feel that drawing a simple scenario may assist to clear my point.

> "A diabetic is diagnosed by a specialist as requiring an amputation at the ankles because the feet have been poisoned and may cause further bodily damage. When the specialist surgeons retire to celebrate a job well done after a successful operation, they are then recalled to now amputate the limbs at the knees. It tells them some things never stop."

Apartheid was never designed to end, nor to be understood and cured. There were many victims of apartheid. Some told their stories to others. Many still walk with bullets in their bodies. Some of these were shot while innocently walking in a crowd, which the apartheid police attacked and shot at, claiming that it was an illegal gathering. Such victims could not go to the same police to report or go to doctors or hospitals, knowing that state agents would be waiting for them there. They would feel safe to tell their stories when the ugly storm settled down. For me this is the time.

My story as a black policeman in the apartheid era has always cried out to be told and be known. It is about what I heard, saw and did in the South African Police Force of that era. I got there ten years after the National Party took over government. I remained there for 33 years. I was privileged to participate in the whole life and demise of apartheid. And I harbour no regrets about it. I feel it was a journey worth taking. It is a journey that had its ugly and painful moments.

This book gives a blow-by-blow and step-by-step account of the other side of apartheid era policemen in South Africa as seen and told by one who was there and saw it all.

I hope what I have said above does not, in the eyes of others, make me a pessimist, hard to forgive and one against reconciliation. I am by nature a humble and forgiving person. I have been forgiven by many people along my way. I cannot be the one to deny it to those who deserve it. Racism, to those who live by and for it, seems to be their last strong hold; shedding it completely would leave them stripped of that which gives them entitlement to despise and revile others on the basis of skin colour. The colour factor is there to stay. It demands humility; courage and magnanimity to embrace the human colours that inhabit this part of the universe and make them work for us.

Racism is a phenomenon of human creation and can only be rectified by honest human effort. Though deep-rooted as it is, it is not beyond uprooting. Maybe uprooting sounds harsh and unrealistic. However, fazing it out and getting humankind totally cleansed of it may sound better. It needs us human beings to remove the cataracts from our eyes to see how beautiful blended colours of all races can be.

This book is not only about apartheid and racism. It is about my working life as a policeman and what it gave me in terms of the knowledge gained from working with the mixture of people my work demanded. For me, it was an interesting eye-opener and empowering in many ways in my life.

PART 1
Entry into the Police Force

Chapter 1
The Journey Begins

Perhaps it was that moment on winter's day on a train journey from Johannesburg to Durban, when I lifted my Ilanga Lase Natal newspaper and saw the advertisement that the South African Police was on a recruitment drive for native police recruits, that fate ushered me into the apartheid police force - for the explicit purpose that I feel now after 33 years - to emerge a better informed and empowered person. I was ushered into a vast terrain of all sorts of possibilities where there was enough time to search and perhaps find out who I really was, and which of the characteristics I had that made for a complete human being.

From that day, I was embarked on a journey in a world characterized by fear of dangers, real and imagined. It was a world of extremes. It was sometimes harsh and uncompromising, strewn with shuttered hopes, calculating opportunists, hardened survivalists and unrelenting believers in victory.

I had just left Robinson Deep Gold Mines where I worked as a checker, what some called a junior clerk. I was on my way to visit my mother who worked as a domestic servant in Durban on the Bluff. I was on leave and planned to return to the mine in three weeks' time.

I had bought all the newspapers of that day, except the ones in Afrikaans and had a good time enjoying the newspapers in my third class compartment. As I read the papers, I enjoyed watching, through my window, houses, villages and trees flitting past as the train gained speed with the wheels and the rail line joints giving a rhythmic sound, as part of the entertainment a train had to offer.

When I had time to gather my thoughts, I was 'reminded' of the fact that, when I arrived in Durban, things would be different. I knew that, from the time I disembarked from the train, I faced the likelihood of being stopped by the police and asked to account for my being there. I had no permit to enter Durban, even though I was employed in Johannesburg. I felt very vulnerable.

I would have to tip -oe my way to Cato Manor Police Station, where I wanted to see my former school friend, Thomas Mbhele, who was then a detective there. I wanted to ask him how I would proceed if I had to present myself to the recruitment officer at the

Durban West District Head Quarters in Ridge Road, and make my application to join the force. There was also the question of getting to the Bluff where my mother was. It meant I would avoid the police only when I was on a train or a bus. Police were everywhere, in police vans and on foot; some were on motorbikes and while others rode bicycles. I felt almost trapped. As a native, apartheid prevented me from travelling anywhere in the cities or towns without a permit. If I were to be stopped by the police, I would face arrest and deportation.

    I left my luggage in the cloak room at the Durban main station and got into a Durban Corporation bus to Chesterville. I got off at Cato Manor Police Station, where I met my friend, Thomas Mbhele. He was very happy to see me after a long time and to hear that I too wanted to join the police force. He expressed his wish that I be stationed at Cato Manor so that we could work together and relive our old friendship which had been very cordial before we parted ways. We did not have time to cover any intimate details or broader aspects of police life. He did not discuss positive or negative experiences which he might have gone through so far in his short police career. Perhaps he felt it would be unfair for him to dampen my spirit if I were to learn about the negative aspects of policing or he might have thought there would be enough time to share those aspects with me should I be successful in my application and, with any luck, be stationed with him in Cato Manor or the neighbouring Mayville Police Station.

Chapter 2
My Recruitment

I was in high spirits when I left Thomas, my school time friend at Cato Manor Police Station, to go to the Durban West Police Headquarters on Ridge Road. I had had a happy re-union with a friend who fully shared my hopes of a successful recruitment session with the recruitment officer. It would be my first gateway to a dream, now fired up by my friends' own anticipation of good times ahead for both of us, especially if I were to be accepted and eventually posted to Cato Manor and to the detective branch.

I got to Ridge Road by bus and went straight into the recruiting office having been shown in by the young, white receptionist who spoke to me in Afrikaans. When I responded in English, she seemed comfortable though. Of course the conversation went no further than my asking for the office of the recruiting officer.

With her attitude, I began to hope for a relaxed reception. When I entered the office, the recruiting officer was not there. The receptionist then showed me a bench and told me to wait there.

The officer soon arrived and I stood up and greeted him. He did not indicate that I should sit down. He then went on to enquire if he could help me, yet another relief for me, as he did not say, "What do you want?" I introduced myself and told him that I had come to apply to join the police force and that I had seen an advertisement in a newspaper about the recruitment drive for native policemen. He walked towards the door and asked me to follow him, which I did, thinking that he was leading me to another office where the actual recruitment process would begin.

I began to wonder when we walked up to the street pavement and he checked to see if I was following him. I was now worried and shaken, thinking that he was going to show me the road and mercilessly watch my dream crash. He stood on the pavement and looked down the road. He then pointed to a shopping complex, some eight hundred meters away, and said that I should go to that supermarket and buy a writing pad and an envelope, come back, write my application for recruitment, place the letter in the envelope, and hand it over to him.

I breathed a sigh of relief that he was not chasing me away.

As I headed to the complex, I got the impression that he derived pleasure and satisfaction in watching me walk a distance of about eight hundred meters only to purchase a pen, paper and an envelope while there was plenty of writing paper on his desk. I would have done this with no need to place the application in an envelope but hand it to him as he was the recruiting officer. His whole attitude made me feel that he was not enthusiastic about recruiting blacks into the police force, but was not in a position to stop or prevent it. All he could do was to make the process of that effort as rocky and uncomfortable to black applicants as he possibly could. He also seemed so unconcerned about what kind of a recruit the police force was looking for because he did not bother to ask any questions, even to find out if, as an applicant, I was of a sound mind.

Once I was done, he read my application and told me to call again on a date I was to be taken to the District Surgeon on Smith Street to be examined. There was no gesture of a welcome, nor was there ever a smile.

The whole encounter with the recruitment officer was cold and impersonal. This then was my first point of contact with the police organization of that time and my first experience of a cockiness of attitude revealed contempt, arrogance and what I felt was deep-seated jealousy against the prospect of sharing the title *policeman* with the likes of me. In my view, I was, to him, an example of a loophole or a weak point in the supposed tight rope, protecting, what in the lives of those it affected, was the glaring point of the epitome of the evils that men did.

I inwardly speculated that, to him, the force was sacred ground and home to Afrikaans-speaking youth from orphanages around the country; youth who, for the first time and later throughout their lives, would be in the forefront in the implementation of the laws of apartheid, wreak vengeance for their hopelessness as in-mates of orphanages upon the hopeless blacks, whether they were innocent civilians or policemen.

That therefore was my first glance at what was became my rocking journey through the minefield of being a black policeman in the apartheid police force for 33 gruelling years.

However, I also cautioned myself against making too much of the officer's behaviour because I asked myself how I could know if this was part of checking my patience and discipline. That was the only way I could justify his behaviour in my mind. Eight hundred metres could not have caused me any harm anyway. I still had hard mental and physical training ahead of me anyway. I had to hope my youth and physical fitness would take care of that.

*****

Back in Robinson Deep Gold Mine, I had become an ardent reader of detective books and had become a fan of detective novel authors like Lesley Charteries and many others. Consequently, I developed deep interest in becoming a detective. In the context of the South African Police, detectives were regarded as an elite, group, operating quietly and always attired like gentlemen. In the minds of many, detectives were associated with sharp intellects and smart moves in executing their duties.

Though I had not thought of any possibility of one day becoming a detective, the interest created by the detective novels I had read with so much fervour became a constant dream flickering in the dark distance like a hopeless fantasy. To think that I would one day perform the awesome things I had read about in detective books was an overwhelming thought and just too much of a good dream to come true. It was a vision which I did not want to dwell on. The possibility of such a miracle unfolding in front of me at that time was very distant. I felt I was too far from that kind of honour. I took into account my emergence from a junior mine clerk position, with a lousy salary of pennies per day. Cheap labour was all the mines were about. No other institution could boast of better cheap labour or more exploitative practices than the South African mines. Then again, the worst could be farm labourers tottering on the brink of full scale slavery. In my reality, I believed that it would take a miracle for me to join the police force.

As I sat in the train reading the Ilanga Lase Natal newspaper I was reminded of one of my old teachers who emphasized the importance of reading. He would say, "read, read and read again." He would say that even the old newspapers found in the toilets when there was no toilet paper for blacks, had to be read before use because something in them might appeal to the user to preserve for reference one day. That lesson lodged permanently in my mind.

From the time I started working, I bought newspapers on a daily basis, when they were available. In terms of the wealth of information to which I was exposed, I never looked back. That particular day on the train from Johannesburg to Durban was the result of the adoption of the policy of reading, thanks to my old teacher. May his soul rest in peace.

By the way, I have had the extraordinary luck of having been taught by teachers who were dedicated and gifted. They were real masters of their craft, and oozed innovation. They taught as if it was their utmost aim to stamp an indelible mark on the whole being of every learner. In my case, it indeed worked for them exactly as it appeared was their aim. I can testify to their success.

If I were to trace my passage through their extremely capable hands, I would vividly remember each and every one of their wise words. Their words have carried me through the hazards and successes in the journey of my life. They seemed bound and driven by a collective pact to go beyond the ordinary call of duty. They set out to register their own culture of excellence in their daily lives, and to hold the hand of every learner who showed a thirst for knowledge and a place in the sun. For me personally, they did not only show the way to greener pastures, but also how to get there and stay there.

Chapter 3

From the Durban Station to the Bluff

I returned to the Durban train station to retrieve my luggage. I boarded a bus to the Bluff where my mother was a domestic servant, working for an Afrikaans-speaking family, the Mullers. Apartheid was a very strange animal, as were the complexities surrounding it as my reception affirmed.

I was on leave from my checker/clerical work on the Robinson Deep Gold Mine and was visiting my mother who had been very worried about my being in Johannesburg and so far away from her. I was her only son. My father had passed away two years earlier. When I entered the gate where she worked, Mrs. Muller saw me first and excitedly called out to my mother to come and see. When I proceeded to the servants' quarters in the backyard, where my mother lived, she was very excited and screamed with uncontrollable joy. She cried and cried until I could not hold my own tears.

My spirit lifted farther towards heaven when Mrs. Muller joined in with her own tears of joy. They praised God for answering their prayers. We all knelt on my mother's bed and prayed. Mrs. Muller prayed in Afrikaans while my mother prayed in Zulu. They were both thanking God for my surprise visit; I heard them say, "God we have knelt beside this bed day and night asking you, good Lord, that one day you would surprise us by seeing him enter this gate, and you, good Lord, have done just that today".

It struck me that they had been praying together in my mother's room. How long? I could not tell. However, I had not imagine their combined trust in God and also how they demonstrated their freedom from that which chained people to beliefs of division, rather than love and respect for humankind.

I cried because that heavenly moment was awesome and overwhelming to me. Mrs. Muller, an Afrikaans-speaking woman, and her employee, my lowly domestic servant mother, were both immersed in a spiritual union. Their unrestricted passion etched an indelible mark on my mind.

Throughout my life as a policeman, apartheid played a pivotal role in my ability to look at the world and South Africa, in particular. I had a life-sustaining belief that along this whirlwind there would be episodes of revelations of the good and evil in hearts. This was the time of the ideology of forced separateness and the beginnings of the entrenchment of cancer of apartheid.

That episode of the spiritual encounter under the umbrella of a celestial power in my mother's room in the homestead of the Mullers, also taught me something. The institutionalized separation of races by the apartheid government did not render all Afrikaans-speaking people heartless and cruel. However, it was meant to serve them better than all the other races. Others were God fearing true Christians like the Mullers, who, it could be said, had their hearts in the right places and who travelled the spiritual world guided by a torch of compassion and colour-blind humanness.

Chapter 4
The Security Branch Interview

In the course of the recruitment process, I was instructed to go to the offices of the Security Branch which were then also referred to as the Special Branch where I was interviewed by two black members of the force. The interviewers seemed intent on finding out where, if anything at all, my political interests lay. I sailed clearly away from all pitfalls along that route.

I had a very clear understanding of the political terrain in the country at that time. I was an ardent newspaper reader and I had my political role models in the local and African scenarios of that time. I found the interview interesting because the questions they asked were such that one could easily read their intent. Whoever prepared the questions really undermined them as well as the recruits they interviewed. For instance, in the political turmoil that was taking place with the Nationalist government enforcing apartheid and political leaders getting arrested and banned, I felt it most naive and absurd for them to ask me if I knew of Chief Albert Luthuli. I observed the two men breathe a sigh of relief when I said I had never heard of him. I said if he was a politician, I was not interested in politics.

However, later, when I was inside the police force, and the thought of that interview came up, I realized why those members expressed relief when I had declared no interest in politics. I assume, it was because they felt I had to be given an opportunity to get the job. If I had answered otherwise, I would have put them in a situation where they could not help me join the force. In the game of spying, as far as they were concerned, I could have been a member of the Special Branch from elsewhere, who had come to entrap them.

Chapter 5
Police Training

It came time came to proceed to the police training college in Wentworth. We were all black recruits assembled there, some coming from as far as the Free State and all over Natal (now Kwa Zulu-Natal). It was an exclusively black recruits' training course.

The place seemed to have been an old army barracks converted to a police training college for blacks. We were shown our rooms, which had doors facing each other and separated by a long passage.

The roof was flat and made of cement. We would get to know later that the roof was also used to patrol those serving certain kinds of punishment. They were called roof guards. Each recruit occupied a room on his own. We were warned that the doors of each room had to be kept open throughout the night so that the sergeants doing inspection rounds did not have to knock on and open so many doors.

The lights stayed on during the night. It was such a strange and awkward situation, completely without privacy and seemingly meant to make the recruits' lives as unpleasant as possible. On the whole, the place was clean, and there was no reason to complain about the food served, although it was nothing to write home about.

Having read books on military training and other tough training courses pertaining to defence or security matters, and having heard stories from others who had undergone the training, we never expected police training to be a walk in the park. We had made up our minds that if there was a bullet to bite, we were ready for the exercise. There was no going back. If that was the test to prove our credibility, responsibility and fitness to grapple with whatever life threw at us, then that was a challenge we had accepted to prove our skeptics wrong.

We were told that we were lucky because, when we arrived, we found the college empty. The group before us had completed their course, gone through their passing out parade and left a few days before ours began. We were told that had we found them still in the place, they would have taken us through a traditional initiation period, which involved severe ill treatment; a kind of hazing. This included, amongst other things, no sleeping at night, and being ordered into the parade ground which was inside the barracks enclosure. Our predecessors would have acted as our instructors, pretending that they were teaching us to drill and do physical training. And because we were new, we would not have been aware that they were not instructors, but newly qualified police recruits waiting to be posted to their new stations of work. There would have been nobody to complain to because, after five o'clock, the official instructors and administration staff would have closed the gates and left. We were told that the strange thing was that, even when those mistreated reported what those seniors awaiting departure did to them by the way of ill treatment, the real instructors and officials seemed to make it a laughing matter.

All this was intended to let everyone know that life was going to be tough during training. It seemed to be in their interests to have the recruits live in constant terror throughout the course. We supposed that, if that was a way of preparing us for the tough times ahead in our police careers, perhaps, it all made sense.

The training college staff included the college commander, a tall, slender and elderly white Afrikaans-speaking unapologetic racist. He did not spend a day without throwing racial tantrums and insults at the black recruits. He had a particular dislike for Zulu recruits and would allude to the fact that they did not speak Afrikaans and were therefore stupid. He preferred those who spoke fluent Afrikaans from the Free State and Transvaal. He would often make jokes about Zulus. His favourite jest was that Zulus feared the letter 'R' like a snake because, to them, all R's L's. For example, a lorry was a 'loli' and Robert was 'Lobethi'.

There was a Xhosa recruit that the commander appeared to hate so much that, when he could not master a certain part of the drill, the commander would shout at him saying, "that's what education does to a bloody kaffir." This same recruit prided himself on the good English he spoke, which sometimes confused the same instructor and brought the officer's annoyance and hatred to a boiling point.

This commander also spoke some Zulu. He thought he spoke the language well but this, in fact, was not the case. Despite that, he would make himself understood in Zulu.

The black English speaker he hated was subjected to all kinds of disciplinary action and punishment, the most common being nights on roof patrol. Up to the time we completed our course, this recruit was still serving one of his roof guard punishments which ended on the day of the passing-out parade.

The second in-charge, a lecturer, was a young Afrikaans-speaking white man. He was a good lecturer, and did not display any particular position with respect to race. He would not qualify as a 'liberal' either and could not display dislikes or objections to the commander's extreme racism. We did not expect him to challenge his commander's behaviour. But someone who harboured such objections and dislikes would have had a way of showing it to us without exposing himself. He never did.

There was a junior white member of the college staff, a young Afrikaans-speaking man who seemed to have no particular duty, except visiting troupes at the drill training grounds. He never had anything much to say and his most important characteristic was that he was never neither laughed nor smile in front of recruits. If anything forced him to laugh, he would turn his back and walk away, appearing bent on sharing the laughter with himself. When he barked drill instructions, he did it with such authority and energy that the recruits felt that he must have had some army training at one point in his life. He was nicknamed 'Yellow Dog'. How and why he got that name, we did not know.

Then came the black instructors. There were five of them in our course. Two were Sesuthu-speaking from the Eastern Cape, the former Transkei, and another one was from Umthata. The fourth one had the surname of a coloured person and we did not know where he came from. A physical training instructor, from Lamontville Township, was the fifth member of the 'black squad'.

All the black drill instructors, including the one who spoke Afrikaans were former soldiers. All were strict disciplinarians, with the exception of the one from Umthata, who was, by nature, a kind person. He was, however, an expert drill instructor in our course.

The physical instructor was also a very friendly and good instructor, and had been an amateur boxer in his earlier years. He was what one could call 'streetwise' as well, because he quickly brought in line and got the respect of those who came from townships and were inclined to display an attitude that undermined others, 'undermining attitude'.

Our good-natured and brilliant drill instructor had an addiction to horse racing, and he attended horse racing events every Saturday. During drill training there would be breaks for rest. During those breaks he would approach every recruit on parade in his troupe and ask them what they dreamt during the night. Whatever a recruit told him, he would then find time to analyze and interpret the dream in terms of horse numbers. Sometimes he would come and report that some of the dreams he interpreted to race horse numbers and races resulted in wins. The routine continued; it was always back to checking dreams again.

All this did not affect his focus on instructing a winning troupe. I was a counter in our troupe, because during the search for counters, I was found to have a clear voice. Being a counter was very simple. It involved counting from one to three, For instance, when an instructor approached the parade (a lined up troupe), he would shout 'Parade!' and the counter would shout 'one, two three, one,...', and members would stand at attention.

Part of our physical training required us to take a long distance road walk which started from the training college at the western bottom of Wentworth, just opposite Clairewood racecourse, to Brighton Beach. The section at the beach was quite a tough one because of the steep winding climb from the engine oil refinery to the Brighton Beach main road and down to the beach. I was very scared of the road walk because when I joined I was very much overweight. Indeed, my unusually heavy weight had nearly disqualified me during recruitment. This happened during the medical examination when the district surgeon struggled to pinpoint my veins from which to draw blood for laboratory tests. He had to prick my forearm several times before he could find the right vein, something that made him lose his temper. He cursed me and sent me packing. He could not take the embarrassment of being an experienced doctor who failed to find a vein from which to draw blood.

Because I was working hard during physical training and had lost a reasonable amount of weight before we moved on to road walks, I managed to cover the distance to and fro without any trouble. In fact, at one time, I was paraded in front of all the other recruits and praised for my dedication and hard work to lose weight.

We attended lectures on the Police Act, statute laws, powers of arrest, common law, police rules and regulations. The emphasis, however, was on discipline, complete loyalty and strict obedience.

We were taught that every white policeman was a superior to every black policeman; that a white recruit of a day in the police force could give instructions and expect obedience from a black policeman thirty years his senior in age and service.

This policy was very controversial and difficult to accept, and the recruits simply listened. They understood that the purpose of the lecture was to sink the policy deep in the minds of the black student policemen with all the emphasis and enthusiasm. However, the recruits never accepted the policy at heart. Instead, there was resentment against the policy that remained embedded in the minds of the recruits. This was a first chapter of what was to be the true colours of apartheid within the police force.

The apartheid club had no intention of hiding or disguising their intentions, however gory and sinister the intentions were. As long as it was blacks who were adversely affected, the gruesome outcomes of apartheid had no effect on white consciences. In apartheid, the toxin of hatred towards blacks coursed through white veins. Whites wished for and forced themselves to believe blacks were non-humans anyway.

Sometimes one felt it strange that such powerful brains (because some of them really were 'brainy'), could drift into and be swallowed by a hypnotic world governed by hate; a world that sealed them away from realism, rationalism and from seeing and hearing clear warning signs ordinary right thinking people could see and hear clearly. Even if one were successfully brainwashed, to resign oneself to and reluctantly accept the idea that perhaps racism was meant to be, there would still be the problem of suppressing irritability and resistance?

Racists derived pleasure in needling and seeing the recipients of their racist actions squirm and limp from the hurt inflicted.

Chapter 6
Starting as a Constable Recruit

I worked in private clothes with uniformed members. There was a police barracks in Mayville where we were accommodated in the native section. There was also a section in the same building for white single policemen.

As a non-uniformed recruit, I was never expected to walk a beat alone. As such, I would be paired with a uniformed black policeman to patrol or walk the beat in the area. I would listen to black policemen talk among themselves about how they were being discriminated against. Black policemen were the majority in the station and they were the only ones walking the beat under the supervision of by black and Indian sergeants.

A white sergeant and his crew drove the relief's patrol van with a white constable sitting with him in the front, while a black constable sat alone in the back. They would occasionally visit the beats to check if the walkers and the supervising sergeants were doing their work properly.

The routine was that the policeman who walked the beats would stop to rest at certain points for about five minutes. He would note the time and point in his pocket books and then move on. The streets he covered on his beat were recorded. If, for instance, he was sent to walk beat six, the roads, avenues and streets he covered were well defined, as well as the points. If the sergeant found him not walking the beat according to instructions, or not leaving one point in time to reach the second point at the correct time, the supervising sergeant would demand policeman's pocket book and make an entry. The entry would state that the member failed to walk his beat according to the rules. The supervisor would also make an identical entry in his own pocket book . Later, when the supervisor reached the charge officer, he would then make a report in the occurrence book about the member. The member would later be called in to a hearing to answer the charge.

Indian constables and sergeants used to work in the charge office dealing with incoming complaints. The office registered prisoners, checked the holding cells and fed those waiting for trial. Sometimes a black policemen worked in the charge office, assisting in taking statements from black complainants who could not speak English.

The charge office sergeant usually was a senior white sergeant who oversaw the smooth running of the relief's work. The set up in terms of duty allocations was not exactly the same at all police stations. There were police stations where whites as well as Indians walked the beat. It appeared to be left up to station commanders as to who worked where and did what at their stations. Even the police stations in the black townships had white officers and sergeants as station commanders. There were also detective branches in the stations. White commissioned officers or senior sergeants ran all these.

There was a lot of illiteracy within the black and Indian policemen, especially the older ones. I remember one night when I was on beat duty and skipped a page in my pocket book by mistake. I asked an old Indian sergeant when he visited me on my beat as to what I had to do to explain the skipping of the page. He said, I should just write 'skip narrow'. Since I could not understand what he meant, I went to ask a white sergeant for clarification. He said that I should draw a straight line across the unwritten page and write, 'skipped in error'.

Chapter 7
The Cato Manor Riots

One afternoon I returned from town to the Cato Manor police barracks. I was shocked to find one of the station's raiding trucks off-loading dead policemen. People and policemen were standing in groups in front of the police station. It was said that the police were killed by mobs of people in the Cato Manor Township, known as Mkhumbane.

There was no one in the mood to tell what had happened. Instead, there was a lot of tension, anger, and sadness.

It was the first time that so many policemen had been killed while on duty in what was then called Natal Province. The word on the street was that the police were carrying out their usual raids for illicit liquor in the township when they were attacked by a mob of township people and were hacked by all kinds of other weapons, including bush knives. Some people were arrested as suspects.

I did not have the opportunity to be near the situation to get to know what exactly happened.

When the police officers were off-loaded from the trucks, a major who spoke in Zulu was heard to say, ***"zizobuya lezizinduku"*** meaning "these deaths will be avenged."

*****

One morning, there was a protest march from Cato Manor against the detention of Inkosi Albert Luthuli. The marchers were demanding that Luthuli be released from prison and they intended to get to the Durban Central Prison where they thought he was detained. Police officers came from many police stations around Durban to go and stop the marchers from getting into Durban. The police based themselves at the Cato Manor Beer Hall and declared that no one should pass through the roadblock they had formed. Multitudes of people from Cato Manor and Chesterville were stopped at that point. People were shouting ANC political slogans, such as "we shall follow Luthuli wherever he goes". Lots and lots of people sat on one side of the roadblock waiting, singing and shouting slogans.

It so happened that I was posted to work in the enquiries section in Mayville Police Station. I was working there with a young, white Afrikaans-speaking policeman. Our work involved attending to accidents and working common assault cases. We worked very well together and the question of racism had no part in our relationship.

He seemed to have been brought up in a home where there was respect for blacks.

As stations had to prepare food and take it to the policemen manning the roadblock, my white colleague and I were told to join the Mayville Barracks kitchen staff to prepare food and deliver it. We prepared sandwiches and tea or coffee which we packed in large cardboard boxes, loaded into a police van and delivered to the roadblock.

For white policemen, we were instructed to make sandwiches with white bread, butter and jam. For blacks it was brown bread and jam. Whenever we delivered the food at the roadblock, the white policemen lined up first and took their food while the blacks waited. We did this for three days.

On the third day, we got to the roadblock late with the food which was meant to be breakfast. We had always delivered it around eight o'clock. When we got there, the white policemen were very angry and rushed to get the food. They ate all their white bread sandwiches. Soon, they were going to eat the brown sandwiches meant for the black policemen.

This became a very hot issue with the black policemen. They complained that they were unfairly treated. They asked what would happen if a situation requiring their attention arose, and they were unable to give it sufficient attention because they were hungry. We went back and prepared food for them. When we returned the white policemen still wanted to partake in the food intended for the black policemen.

*****

The police drew a line at the roadblock separating them from the protesters from the Cato Manor. The police had warned that those who ignored the warning and crossed the line would be shot. Nevertheless, the crowds kept threatening to force their way through.

The mood was extremely tense and confrontational. The police stood in a line across the road on their side with caspers and Saracens behind them.

The waiting game at the "war zone" lasted a full 24 hours. The police were armed to the teeth, with fingers itching to pull the trigger. They actually cursed the fact that the protestors were not aggressive to a point where they could be given an order to mow them down.

Most black policemen prayed in silence that the protestors did not take the bait, and thus provoke their own massacre. Black policemen in that situation were faced with a huge dilemma. Most of them were citizens of Mkhumbane-Cato Manor. The marching protestors were their wives, children, relatives and neighbours. They found little relief only in the fact that they were not armed with any form of guns. That way they would be spared having the blood of their own people on their hands should the shooting happen.

If the white policemen had started shooting at the protestors, the black policemen would have had no role to play. The black policemen ran the risk of being shot themselves, even deliberately, by their white colleagues.

The distrust that prevailed was manifested by how the black policemen were armed, with sticks. Meanwhile, while white policemen were armed with stern guns, shot guns, .33 rifles, revolvers and pistols.

Clearly, black policemen did not want to be armed in the same way, to be part of a massacre of their own people.

As well, black policemen were frustrated by the way black people were treated. White policemen knew that the black policemen did not like what the white policemen did to black people, including black policemen and probably this gave them some sick pleasure.

The day after we delivered food late to the policemen at the roadblock, a shocker to the white policemen happened. It became such a moving issue that it widened the gap of distrust between the black and the white policemen. It became a matter for discussion among all policemen in riot situations.

On this particular morning, women bringing food to the protestors at the roadblock (because the protestors too stayed there for 24 hours and they had to be fed) brought food for the black policemen as well. It was not brown slices of bread with jam but steaming pots of curry, rice and chicken, which they washed down with *Amahewu* (a thirst quenching drink made from melie-meal).

The women lined up the pots in the space between the police and the protestors and invited the black policemen to partake. The food was so appetizing and mouth-watering, served in such attractive crockery, with stainless steel knives and folks that the whole lunch period at the roadblock turned into a five-star hotel treatment for the black policemen. A senior white policeman tried to stop the black policemen from participating, but they refused and went on to enjoy the food.

The protestors were also telling the policemen that they were not fighting to liberate themselves; they knew that the black policemen were oppressed and discriminated against, as had been demonstrated previously on that roadblock. They were saying this in English, targeting the ears of the white policemen.

As events unfolded, some officers came to witness what was happening and, after that, the black policemen were called on parade. They were addressed by a high-ranking white officer who tried to tell the black policemen that they were taking a risk, eating food provided by the protestors. "What if the food was poisoned?" he asked.

The black policemen just laughed and the senior officer accused them of being drunk from liquor they were given by the women protestors. A black policeman, who was indeed intoxicated, swore at the officer, saying it was he (the officer) who was drunk. The police officer ordered that the policeman be taken to the police station and be detained.

Had the black policeman not been intoxicated, there would have been serious trouble for the other black policemen, because they would have staged their own protest in his support. It did not become an easy issue for the white senior policemen because the white policemen who had eaten the food meant for the black policemen, in front of the protestors, created a shameful situation. This incident united the black policemen with the protestors and won their sympathy. Some of the protestors were shouting and saying: "We are protesting for you as well because in Chief Luthuli's government you will never be treated like that". They continued to say: "You brothers do not belong on that side of the line; you belong to the people." Then they would shout the slogan, **"iAfrika mayibuye"**, let Africa return to Africans.

This also became a talking point in the townships and the black policemen themselves engaged in a lot of soul searching. Others even contemplated resigning and joining the people.

*****

The protests spread to other townships around Durban. I was called up to join other policemen who drove around in big trucks. We were instructed to go to spots where marching took place. Buses were stopped by the people from taking anyone to work. While driving in a convoy of trucks through Marrianhill, about three o'clock one morning, we came upon a number of black men digging a trench across the road to prevent buses from going into town.

They were surprised as they were caught red-handed while they were busy digging the trench. They thought our trucks were buses which they intended to prevent from passing. Soon after they were apprehended, they were ordered to fill up and cover the trench.

As they were covering the trench, some white policemen were kicking and swearing at them. They called us (black policemen) to come along and help refill the trench. We found extra spades lying around which seemed to indicate that other diggers were still coming to join in the effort, but they had probably turned back when they realized that we were policemen. While we were helping to fill up the trench, the white policemen who were standing behind the suspects, kicking and swearing at them, started ordering us as if we were suspects too, shouting, "come on, come on."

We stopped helping and threw our spades on the ground. When some of the suspects saw that, they took the opportunity to run away. This incident created a further problem between the white and the black policemen. A senior sergeant came to resolve the matter and we all drove along with the remaining suspects after they had filled the trench.

We proceeded to Clermont Township where there was a big protest march and sloganeering by crowds, saying they were marching to the central prison to fetch Luthuli.

The police positioned themselves at the Clermont bus rank at the entrance to the township. People came along all roads leading to the main rank and from all sections of the township. Policemen (black and white) had come in the police trucks to the place of the riots.

When the police saw the people coming and gather at the rank, a white sergeant spoke over the loud-howler, calling for an interpreter to come forward to order the people to disperse. He was looking at the large group of black policemen who were there.

There was no response from the black policemen. When the white policemen felt the urgency to order the people to leave, they shouted over the loud howler in English but the people did not respond. Instead, the crowds were multiplying into larger numbers.

When the officer with the loud-howler shouted, "I will count up to three, and you will be forcefully removed from here," there were more noises of songs and slogans.

The officer then started counting and when he reached three, ordered, "disperse them" and the police attacked the crowd with baton sticks. The people ran in different directions in the township.

They were chased deep into the township, whilst being beaten up. Black policemen just chased and did not assault anyone.

When the police returned to their base at the bus rank, the protestors started regrouping.

It was at that point that a white senior sergeant called the black policemen to attention. He addressed us saying that they (whites) had noticed that we were not beating the people and therefore we were not complying with instructions. As he spoke, he was standing almost in front of me.

I caused trouble for myself when I said that we complied with instructions and removed people from the bus rank.

He asked, "How?"

I said that we had chased them away.

All the officers, including high-ranking ones, turned to look at me and I was ordered to stand in front. The sergeant then, in a manner that showed he was gearing up for a 'David and Goliath' debate, which he was sure to win, sort of collected himself and said, "Now that I see you speak English, why did you not come forward when we called for an interpreter?"

I calmly said, "it was because I am not an interpreter."

He hissed the word, "you are not a what?"

I sensed that they were collectively and corroboratively seeing insolence in my response. I tried to navigate my response quickly into calmer waters by saying, "when we left the station and when we got here, nobody was identified and told that when the need arose for an interpreter to be used, he would be the one, as was usually the case when people of other races were to be addressed."

He put on a sarcastic smile behind which a storm of anger was brewing and he said, "do you expect us to say we are sorry we forgot; do you really take us for that?" He looked at the others as if saying, 'people do you see what we are faced with?' It seemed as if he was seeking approval to order that I be arrested on the spot.

I felt that there would be nothing stopping them to do that. I continued by adding that no order had been given to us to beat up anyone; we were ordered to disperse the crowd and when we advanced towards them, they ran away and dispersed.

That infuriated him further into saying, almost shouting, "look here, my boy. I have dealt with kaffirs long before you were born, and if you think you are a lawyer, go and practise it somewhere else, not here in the police force."

A senior officer of the rank of Lieutenant went up to the sergeant, whispered something into his ear, and the sergeant disengaged. I did not know what was would happen next.

Just about that time, a group of men walked to the rank carrying a dead man. One of the men addressed the police and said, "you went out game hunting and this is what you achieved. Take your game and go and eat it."

There was dead silence.

A man-about-town of that time, looking sharp and street-wise from Clermont, known as Clerment Shange, came to the rank and addressed the police saying, "you come here in cowardly large groups, armed like that and kill our innocent and unarmed people." From the faces of the white policeman, one could see that they felt that that was the worst provocation they had ever received from a black man. Clerment went on and said, "I challenge any of you who thinks he is fit enough to come forward and let us have a go; if you defeat me, arrest me for assault or attempted murder if you want to."

Many had their fingers on their triggers praying for an order to shoot him. I thought the senior officer was wise not give an order to shoot in front of so many witnesses.

*****

Before we left Clermont Township, I was called aside by three well-known and respected citizens who were standing in front of Zondis' Tea Room watching the whole thing. They said that they wanted the black policemen who were there to know that they had noticed that they did not beat up people as the people fled, and for that they were thankful. These men were Mr. Mswazi Dlamini, who was a boxing trainer and a friend of mine, Nonkomfela Ndelu, a shop owner and writer, and Makhathini a soccer administrator. As I write, all of these men are now deceased.

Before all the police left Clermont, some of us were taken to a make-shift office in Pinetown for questioning. The group consisted of the late constable Mdletshe of Mayville, Ngcobo, also of Mayville, and two others, whose names I cannot recall. All of us had been involved in the argument at the refilling of the trench in Marrianhill in the early hours of that morning. We were questioned about our supposed insolence and lack of discipline. When I was called in, I found three white middle-aged detectives. They looked angry and determined to make me realize that they were not the uniformed policemen I had been dealing with at the Clermont bus rank. One asked me if I had suddenly felt that I was at the wrong place in the police force. He said that if that was the case, then sooner I left the force, the better for everyone.

One confronted me with the question, "Do you want to serve Verwoerd or Luthuli?" I said. I wanted to serve the government. He shook his head slightly, seemingly to contain an inward explosion that was building up. He repeated, "I said, do you want to serve Verwoerd or Luthuli? Did you hear me mention government?"

I said, "No."

He then continued, "Why do you not want to answer my question?"

At that time I had just joined the police force and I had not yet come across stories of torture and murder by the Security Branch. That kind of police behaviour, however, slowly gathered momentum, and it reached its peak when I was already in the Detective Branch, and when apartheid was at its peak.

I feared mostly that I would be fired if I was thought or found to be disloyal. The way the question was being put to me was awkward, because indeed I did not regard myself as serving either Verwoerd or Luthuli as none of these had government. I was put in a corner to answer the security detective's question the way he wanted, but when he put it again I felt I would be, as far as he was concerned, insolent or confrontational. I said that as far as I knew, Luthuli had no government for me to serve.

He lit a cigarette and dragged one lungful of smoke and slowly released it showing inner satisfaction, seeing himself as a cat playing with a tired rat before it. He was enjoying my inexperience pitted against the vastness of his, and felt he had nicely driven me into a corner where Luthuli had been eliminated and we were just left with Verwoerd. He then pounced. "Well, you say Luthuli has no government, what about Verwoerd's government, what is your problem with Verwoerd?"

I found a gap and answered, "I have no problem with Verwoerd."

He seemed to breathe a sigh of relief and said, "Good!" He went on to say, "I do not want to think you hate Verwoerd like Luthuli's people do, and you know they do. You can see all over the place all the native people[1] are loyal to Luthuli. You have heard them sing that they will follow him wherever he goes. To them it is not as if he has no government as you say. So you must be careful what you say." The one who appeared younger than the other two, asked me to tell them about the drama I created at the Clermont bus rank, trying to display how clever I was in front of members of the

---

[1] Remember I was still a native constable

public, and communists at that. His direct question was, "What did it matter if you had not been appointed as an interpreter if your assistance was required by a unit of which you were a member? If you are a loyal member it was your duty to volunteer assistance, you needed not to be begged or appointed." He went on, "What do you say now that a person has been killed there because you did not help explain to the people that they should disperse?"

I responded by saying that we were being accused of not beating the people when they had been told to disperse and we said that we were told to disperse them and they ran away in different directions as soon as we advanced towards them. I said, if I was against anyone or not loyal I would be telling the press that we, the natives, were being accused by our superiors of not beating up people, even to death, as it happened with the person beaten up by the European policemen (as they were then called).

He took my particulars, made a sign to his colleague and told me to go. I knew that, from then on, my behaviour would be monitored. When we were allowed to go, the others, who were also taken to the Security Branch, said they were questioned about the incident at the trench and they told their questioners that they were also kicked when the European policemen kicked the suspects who had been digging the trench. They said they had objected to that as it was not only demeaning but was a provocation which they could not allow. There seemed to have been no fault in their behaviour and they were not even warned of anything when they were told they could go.

Chapter 8
The Paranoid Sergeant

There was the day I worked at the charge office at Mayville Police Station. I was busy sealing envelopes with sealing wax and a piece of string. I had a roll of string that I used to secure the breadth and the length of the envelope. I would have it in two lines going both ways and make a knot at the centre in the front. I would write the destination address on the back, light the sealing wax, let it melt onto the knot, and press the seal stamp on it, leaving a smart, round imprint.

As I did this, there was a white senior sergeant in the charge office writing the occurrence book. I noticed him watching me with keen interest while I went on with my work with the envelopes. I wondered why he was that much interested in what I was doing.

Eventually, he could not restrain himself any longer from expressing what was on his mind. He shifted his chair to face me directly, and cleared his throat as if to ensure that what he was about to say would be as clear and to the point as possible. He said, "You know what, constable, I have been watching you the whole morning doing what you are doing. Now, you people think we whites are a bunch of monkeys, and you are very wrong."

I was sitting there wondering what the hell he was up to. I was itching to hear him spell out whatever it was in his wisdom that made him think that he had got me in such a corner that I could not miss every one of his sarcastic words meant to be political lecturing.

"Listen carefully now," he said. "I have been watching that roll of string getting smaller and smaller as you eagerly and determinedly made sure that you comply with the orders of your communist bosses, the ANC."

Now I was not only getting scared but also puzzled.

"We know, as you do, that the ANC has sent you people here to implement their desire to bring this government down in every way you can. Look at you; instead of using one line of string over the envelopes you are using two lines. Everybody else uses one line and serves the required purpose, but you, because it's only you and I in this office and you think I am blind or stupid, and think this is a chance you should not miss, to add to the economic boycotts against us."

He was becoming unstable and emotional as he went on to say, "Do you realize that in all your toilets in the station we do not supply you people with toilet paper? Instead, we see that you make do with old newspapers for the simple reason that we know that, in line with what you are doing today, you would make it a point to do the same with those rolls of toilet paper. We also know that when a black man says 'thank you' to a white man in his heart he says f... you, f... you." He firmly added, "I do not want you to explain why you doubled the string because you have no reason and I won't ask you because I know. Next time, no sealing job for you. Next time when you do these for your masters, do not be careless because we are not all fools."

I was flabbergasted and just had no words to say. I feared that he might talk to others about what he thought was his discovery, that day. I did not know whether to continue sealing the envelopes or not. However, while I was still in shock due to his diatribe and undecided as to what to do next, he turned to face his desk turning his back against me and said, "You may continue sealing but one line of string this time, and always especially in my presence."

I nearly said thank you but quickly remembered what he said about 'thank you.' I continued until I finished sealing the enveloped.

In a way, when I thought of it, I was happy that I had awakened the animal in him and his extreme racism was exposed. At least I got to know where I stood with him, and perhaps many of his ilk.

Chapter 9
The Scare of my Life

One late afternoon when I returned to the Cato Manor Police Station and to our police barracks, I received a report, that raised concern, from a black constable working in the charge office at the time. He told me that there was a prisoner in the police cells who wanted to see me. The Constable accompanied me to the police cells and to my great shock, as soon as I got to the cell door I was greeted by the political slogan 'Afrika', shouted by the prisoners who were detained in there – some of them for political activities. In front of these people was my training college friend Gumede who, in our college days, was part of our group that discussed political issues. I sensed that he had been talking favourably about me in the cells to the other inmates and that was the reason for the 'Afrika' greeting when they saw me.

The act was a serious one because of the presence of the police charge office person. I did not know whether he would report the matter to the superiors, or what his reaction would be. He was a young black constable who would have thought the act would be a scoop for him to report.

Gumede told me that he had just resigned from the police force and was picked up for political matters. When I heard it, I was so shocked I did not know how to react. I did not know whether to warn the policeman not to report it or to leave it like that; for on the other hand, the warning would awaken him to the seriousness of the matter which perhaps he had not regarded as such.

That day, I had just arrived at the charge office and I was supposed to proceed to the barracks thereafter.

I changed direction and, instead of proceeding to the barracks, went to the bus stop and boarded a bus to the city and from there to the beach front. I paced back and forth on the beach sands trying to gather my senses together about the whole matter of Gumede and the 'Afrika salute' by his cell mates and him. I did not rule out my own arrest if the constable reported exactly what he heard and saw. I decided to get back to the barracks late and, when I got there, I found the other policemen already in bed. I thought that was better but I still thought it a bad idea to find everybody asleep because I could have, per chance, got information as to whether the matter had gone beyond the charge office constable or not. To my great relief it turned out that it had not.

I had survived a scare of my life.

Chapter 10

Association with a Liberal Party Family

In the mid-sixties, while still stationed at Mayville Police Station, I had occasion to associate with a family who were members of the Liberal Party. They were Mr. Ken Hill and Mrs. Joan Hill of number 27 Meryick Avenue, Mayville. They were a family truly dedicated to give educational assistance to black students privately. They gave this assistance free of charge in their own house, at their own time. They provided us with tea, cakes and biscuits at all our study sessions.

Truly, this was indeed a wonderful couple, wholly embarked on a mission to uplift dedicated students privately. Those in the same group with me were the late Ben Makhaye, who later became a prominent businessman in Umlazi, owning several supermarkets; the late John Majola of Chesterville, who later became an attorney in Durban; Elliazer Mbhele, who later became a property developer; and Sazi Victor Ntuli, who became a successful salesman.

Mrs. Hill did the actual teaching. Ken was a full time lecturer at the Natal University. Because they were members of a political party, I had an uneasy feeling regarding the reaction of the Security Branch once they got wind of my association with the couple. This would potentially be serious considering that the Liberal Party, to which the couple belonged, was totally opposed to apartheid. I might be perceived that I was, in some way, daring the Security Branch to touch me. That was definitely not the case with me.

When I wrote some poetry and submitted it to the late Mr. Allan Paton for his opinion and advice, and we began meeting quite often, he remarked that the Security Branch would have already been aware of our meeting and that they would think that we were sharing state secrets. I told him that as far as I was concerned, they had no grounds for that because they knew that I was nowhere near having access to their secrets. They would know that even if I, a native constable, stumbled upon a stone of state secrets, I would most probably throw it into the river, hating it for tripping me and nearly causing me to fall. I told him that in the eyes of those people I was invisible. I was just as good as a sleeping dog. I knew of no secrets that I could share with anyone, let alone state secrets and with a white leader of a political party known for its opposition to apartheid.

He said I should remember that it would not only be me they would think was passing information to him, but they also would assume he was using what they would think was my vulnerable mind, to change me to see apartheid for what it was and perhaps arm me with political knowledge to do something about it. I agreed with him on this point and stopped calling at his house to discuss my writings with him.

Mrs. Hill taught us no ideology, other than her special subject, English. She would invite students from the medical school on days when she would play one of Shakespeare's plays on gramophone records. Being in the same room with medical students and listening to Shakespeare together was my ultimate joy.

Of all the poetry we dealt with, I was fascinated by the two masterpieces. **Elegy** written in a country churchyard by Thomas Grey and **Ulysses** by Lord Alfred Tennyson.

We were also invited to attend meetings at the University of Natal where the great Anglican Bishop Zulu reported back on his world tours in front of a multiracial audience. Our association with the university, its great conference halls and experiencing a university campus, inspired us with the feeling that we had a foot in the door.

We were introduced to Latin for beginners, which we enjoyed very much under the expert tutelage of Mrs. Joan Hill.

The most important thing to me about the Hills was that, during the entire time of our association with them, there seemed to be no intent on their part to influence us towards supporting the Liberal Party or embracing any political ideology. They had a love for education, and English literature in particular. It seemed that having noted our craving and thirst for the knowledge they had in abundance, they tapped into their deep reservoir of humanness and adopted us as their own with no thought or expectation of material reward of any kind. The benefits we reaped from their free assistance were double in size and value compared to those we got from institutions or individuals who embraced the notion of, 'nothing for nothing' in a soulless world of materialism.

*****

In 1973 there was an invitation from publishers in Britain for English poetry submissions in a book called, **Poetry of the English-Speaking World.** One of my poems titled **Of William Shakespeare and His Friends** was selected and published in that collection. When the article about the poem appeared in the ***Daily News,*** I got a surprise visit from a black member of the Security Branch who said he had just come to congratulate me for giving respect and dignity to black policemen and, in fact, policemen at large. I wondered why the Security Branch was interested in my poetry. I could not get myself to believe that it was an innocent and brotherly visit to share my moment of happiness. Nothing further happened, either from that or the classes at the Hills. I was later transferred to Hillcrest Police Station and could not find time to continue attending classes at the Hills.

PART 2
Colour, Faith and Rank

Chapter 11
The Security Branch

Ordinary policemen like us feared the Security Branch, also known as the Special Branch. They were known for monitoring the movements, attitudes and feelings of the other policemen and black government workers as far as loyalty to the government was concerned. They could detain, torture or even kill those they regarded as a danger to the apartheid government. As such, no one wanted to be in their bad books, because nothing could protect a person if they decided to deal with him. To be in their bad books would be like walking a tight rope, worst of all, if the target were a policeman. They could always claim that such a person abused the trust they had placed upon him; as if they themselves did. We knew clearly that they did not trust black policemen.

The extremist supremacists among the racist police officers did not, by their actions and language, hide that they saw a Dingaan[1] in every Zulu policeman. One could see that, when that moment of history visited, their twisted minds entertained a live picture of the horrific experience of that fateful ride by Piet Retief leaving behind the dead Gerrit Maritz and others in the hands of King Dingaan's warriors, at his great palace. Anything black and Zulu in front of them triggered the exertion of the most venomous hatred stored deep in their dark minds.

Zulus were particularly targeted by the Afrikaans-speaking racists within the police force. King Dingaan's 'unforgivable sin' was at the core of this thinking. It felt, and no doubt was, that now that they were in power, it was **'payback time,'** for 'descendants' of the King. I say these things because I had watched black people who worked in houses, farms and mines under Afrikaans-speaking people. While working under atrocious conditions, those black people did not display any hatred towards their bosses. Instead, they were humble, timid, respectful, and loyal. Indeed, they never tried to organize themselves to resist anything. For some very strange reasons, which were unknown to them, they were hated, despised, and treated like slaves by their 'masters' and 'mistresses'. They were called names, as if all their acceptance of being dehumanized and

---

[1] Dingaan was a Zulu chief who won the throne in 1828 by murdering his predecessor, Shaka, and became notorious for his cruelty.

trampled upon could not help remove King Dingaan's sin.

Ironically, to cap it all, these haters of black people claimed to be God-fearing Christians. I always yearned to see what kind of Bible they read as they religiously attended church every Sunday. It seemed that their bible taught them that they were better than other human beings. I always wondered if their bible had a verse or passage which refers to:

> "Loving your neighbours as yourself" and "Doing to others as you would like to be done to you".

Perhaps, in the narrowness of things, their minds told them that, by neighbours, it meant fellow whites on the farm or house next door. Possibly, if the Bible talked about forgiving those who sinned against them, they took that to mean only if those who sin against them and needed forgiveness were white.

*****

Most black policeman realized that they were ill-treated in the worst ways possible by white policemen. In fact, in many cases, it was even worse than was the case with black members of the public. The most unfortunate experience by the black members of the public was that, while they suffered untold ill-treatment from white policemen and other white people, they also had to deal with ill-treatment from black policemen. This was because some of the black policemen competed with white policemen in the ill-treatment of black members of the public.

I can aver that what some black policemen did to their black brothers and sisters, they never did to other races, such as Indians and coloureds. These black policemen behaved like that in order to impress their seniors; others were just pure morons and sell-outs. Black policemen, who knew that they were doing their best in the police force, would have had nothing to do with those kinds of wayward policemen because they were just as dangerous as some of the white policemen who hated black people. I remember one such black policemen who would have white policemen stand aside and watch him demonstrate how to torture a black suspect. He became a star in the force amongst white policemen who hated blacks.

When we observed that there was no fairness in the way the law worked, especially at the stage when things were still in the hands of the police, and not yet in the courts, we decided to make decisions as to how we would handle our cases. That way, everybody would be treated fairly, and everybody's case fully and well investigated. We had a chance to do that because nobody would have had a reason to stop us from doing the right thing, since the public and the courts wanted cases investigated properly and fairly.

We felt that in order to be supported in what we were doing, we had to approach a political party and discuss with them what we had seen in the police force. We felt that we could change some of the things that took place without exposing ourselves. We were completely against apartheid. We had said that if 'push came to shove' came to that, in our discussions with the African National Congress (ANC), we would consider leaving the police to join the Liberation forces abroad. By 'we' I refer to members of the police with whom we ran the Cato Manor police mess and those with whom we had discussed politics in the training college.

The difficulty was how we were going to approach the ANC. How safe would it be, even to try, given that our own colleagues were watching us, perhaps on instruction by the Security Branch? We were also aware that some members of the ANC were informers of the Security Branch.

We decided to put whomever we chose to approach from the ANC side on surveillance and monitoring first. We would do that when the Special Branch detained black ANC political suspects at the Mayville Police Station. The station had modern buildings and was preferred by the Security Branch for their detainees. Approaching those detainees was difficult because of the instructions from the Security Branch that the apprehended suspects should be handled by white constables, sometimes Indians, for purposes of feeding them, or allowing them to exercise in the courtyard. Black members were not allowed to come into contact with the suspects.

One day, the Security Branch brought their suspect, a black male ANC activist, whom we knew. They had brought him from Lamontville. He was a Law student. They brought him in the evening with all his law books. There were orders to clean his cell and to give him a bed, a mattress and new blankets from the prison store room.

When I saw that, I went to my friends and reported to them my observations. The fact that it seemed like the Security Branch aimed at treating him well, according to me and the group, ruled out the idea of approaching him about our mission. There was consensus that he could be dangerous to our mission. The Security Branch left him there for about two weeks, without getting back to book him out to the interrogation room, or whatever else they had planned to do with him.

We kept on holding our meetings after hours, discussing what racism we had experienced each day at work. Although we were stationed at different police stations, we shared the police barracks at Cato Manor.

One morning, detectives from the Security Branch took their suspect away. They brought him back in the evening and returned to his cell. The following day, his handlers came back to fetch him again. When they returned with him later, there was so much tension that I could easily detect that something had happened at the interrogation room. The Security Branch detective who had brought him back instructed the Indian charge office constable to remove everything from the cell, including the bed, the sheets and the blankets from the cell, as well as the books.

The constable did as he was told and the suspect was then taken to an empty cell and given only a Bible to read. Ordinary prisoners' blankets were brought for him and he was then locked up. Sometime thereafter, he was taken to court, where he was convicted. The day he was dispossessed of his study books and given a Bible to read, it had appeared to us that he had resisted whatever the detectives wanted. We thought that, perhaps, he was the right person for us to approach. Something told us that he could not be associated with the system, least of all their informer.

We came to know when he was released from prison and started his law articles with a law firm in the Valbro Chambers, Victoria Street, Durban. In the Cato Manor Police Station there were law courts that were situated next to our barracks.

One day when I was in court, I saw the law student who had been detained at Mayville, and whom we had targeted to discuss our planned mission. During tea time I approached him, introduced myself and told him that I was a detective stationed at Mayville. I also told him about lawyers who knew me from the courts through my detective work. I had become popular with some lawyers and other court officials because, at that time, I was the only black detective who gave evidence in English while most black detectives gave theirs through interpreters. I told him that I wished to arrange a meeting with him at a time and place of his choice. I indicated to him that there were important matters that could be for the good of our nation that we wanted to discuss with him. He agreed to meet us and gave me a date and time, six o'clock at his office on Victoria Street. Later, I reported the good news to my friends.

We , about five in number, proceeded to his office on the appointed date. At the office, we found an Indian lawyer who asked if he could help us. We insisted that we wanted to see his partner because our matter was rather personal and private. When he pressed us to find out who we were, I told him to tell his partner that I was the person who approached him at Cato Manor court for the meeting and he would remember and he would know who I was.

We were now faced with a stranger who created a risk, as far as we were concerned. Our policy would not allow us to deal with an untested person, especially about the kind of mission we were undertaking. We were disappointed by him (our lawyer friend) for not keeping the appointment with us. We went back to our original suspicion that, likely he was not be totally clean. We decided to leave him alone unless he approached us; he never did. He later went into exile.

Chapter 12
The Homelands

The homelands, or mini-states, in South Africa were meant to fragment black South Africans. The aim was to weaken blacks in their efforts to forge a united front, irrespective of ethnicity, and confront oppression by the minority whites in their advocacy for a free and democratic South Africa.

Those behind the divide and rule philosophy in South Africa knew there would be resistance to the fragmentation. Black South Africans had already formed a political organization in the form of the South African National Congress, ANC. The organization wanted to unite the oppressed, and those who opposed oppression, to create a united democratic South Africa.

Apartheid advocates knew that they could dangle enough carrots to attract a section of the black population to the promised benefits of the homelands. They also knew that those who would swallow the bait would automatically defend those benefits and therefore automatically become allies of the racist system. They figured that in the ensuing confrontations over the issue, blacks would die, likely, in large numbers. The deaths would be at the hands of both the benefactors or collaborators and those who resisted and challenged apartheid. They knew that large-scale elimination of blacks would persist as long as apartheid was foisted upon the black majority in South Africa. It was evident that by dividing blacks and pitting them against one another, it made no difference to them which faction suffered the most casualties as the long-term and central aim of reducing the number of blacks would be accomplished.

The apartheid ideologists used those blacks who participated in their grand scheme as a buffer zone between them and their arch-enemy, the ANC. They took comfort in the thought that the blacks, who collaborated and benefitted from apartheid, would defend it. Those blacks would be thrown into the firing line in a blood bath they (apartheid ideologists) had caused in the first place. The architects of apartheid had forced the idea of homelands upon the majority who had no say in it.

As long as they made sure that the resultant blood bath was at a safe distance from their own doorsteps, and as long as the world did not know the intricacies of that plan, they were happy. While rubbing their hands in glee, they would shrug their shoulders as if giving up on blacks for their stake in turning against one another. They praised themselves for coining a marketable term to the world, calling it black on black violence.

Chapter 13
A Letter to Prince Buthelezi

During the debate on the Bantu Homelands Act, we noted that Prince Mangosuthu Buthelezi was very vocal in his outright opposition and call for rejection of the law. Our group of five used to hold meetings discussing the issue. We were in full support of his stand; we admired him for his courage and wisdom.

He made good use of his academic background and intellectual capacity to articulate his standpoint on behalf of the Zulu Nation, and indeed of all those who stood to lose their South African nationhood in the event of the success of the Bantu homelands idea. He needed the support of all black people whom this policy intended to isolate and enslave. We understood that our situation was perilous should we engage in the debate, specifically because we were all policemen and cared not to be seen to entertain any political inclinations - let alone acting upon them in anyway. Nonetheless, we decided to convey our support, even though he would not know who we were. We, on our part, would remain to savour our patriotic tilt at the granite wall of the evil of that day by supporting Prince Buthelezi. We each entertained a fat hope that one day we would meet our hero face to face and perhaps shake his hand.

We assembled one hot summer day at the lush green lawn in front the southern entrance to the Durban City Hall and wrote a letter in which we praised Prince Buthelezi for his exceptional courage and vision on the issue of the proposed Bantu homelands. We said he was the torch bearer of that resistance. We ended our letter signed, 'Sons of Africa.'

One of our members came from Nongoma, somewhere close to the border of Nongoma and Mahlabathini. He was charged with ensuring that the letter was posted and that it reached the Prince.

From what we had come to understand of the Prince, we felt that he would understand our situation and he would keep our letter in a safe place, while hoping that, one day, he would get to know its authors.

When King Cyprian ka Solomon ka Dinizulu passed away, a friend of mine (who was not one of the authors of the letter) and I went to the king's funeral in Nongoma. We arrived at the king's great palace in the town of Nongoma at the time the mourners had just returned from Mahhashini where the King had been laid to rest.

I was hoping that I would have a glance of Prince Buthelezi, wondering if he had received our letter of encouragement and support and how he felt about it. I knew, as was to be expected, that he would have important people around him to protect and clear his way whenever and wherever he moved. I ruled out the possibility of eye contact with him. I knew that, even though I was the co-author and a secret admirer standing in front of him, he would have had no inkling of who the insignificant commoner was.

At the palace, we were standing in groups in the yard. People were talking about the late king's funeral and seeing friends and exchanging greetings. I could not believe my eyes when I saw Prince Buthelezi moving from group to group, shaking hands with people. When he came towards our group, I felt 'This is it! The moment of truth had arrived.' I felt I would say something to him during the hand shake. I did not know how exactly I was going to do that. I came to a, somewhat, shaky thought that when he shook my hand I would squeeze his so tightly that he would take note and perhaps get annoyed; at the same time I found myself hoping that he would excuse me and dismiss my action as caused by my excitement.

I was lost in my reverie, thinking that I would be squeezing his hand because of my fervent hope that I would have the opportunity in future to remind him of my strange hand shake and explain that it was part of a stupid plan for me to try and introduce myself as a co-author of the letter of praise. I got cold feet and abandoned the idea. I later thought to myself, 'Had I gone on with the strange hand shake and the Prince complained, I would have been declared a wizard out to harm the Prince and deserving of the most horrific death at the hands of frenzied mobs, baying for a drop of my stupid blood.'

A few years later, I found myself realizing and confirming that in fact and indeed miracles do happen. This was when it turned out that the hand shaking episodes for me with the Prince were far from over.

After the Nongoma encounter, a friend of mine came to me with the news that there was going to be a 'welcome home' for the prince when he came from one of his overseas trips and that he was going to address his followers at the Executive Hotel Umlazi. It must have been in the later 1970s. The meeting was planned for the evening. I went there with an agenda of getting close to the prince, hoping yet for a chance to shake his hand. Here I could drop a hint about who I was in terms of the Durban City Hall ground message of praise and appreciation for his honourable stand.

The hall was full and I sat on one of the seats towards the back and close to a window. My friend sat next to me. He was the same friend I had gone to Nongoma with on the day I shook the hand of the prince for the first time.

Prince Buthelezi had this overwhelming aura about him. He was not only a political leader in his own right, but an Inkosi of the Buthelezi clan, whose mother is Princess Magogo, the famous daughter of King Dinizulu. He is cousin to King Cyprian, the father of King Zwelelithini who, a the time of writing, is the reigning King of the Kingdom of KwaZulu. The prince's grandfather was the Prince Minister to King Cetshwayo whose armies defeated the British in the battle of Isandlwana. He is a nephew on the great Kingship of the illustrious history-laden Zulu Nation.

To harbour the hope that I had – that one day I would, while shaking hands with the prince, tell him about the letter – was to me so thin and fragile a prospect, akin to the 'David and Goliath' scenario. Besides, I thought, he may not have received the letter. When I reckoned he often enjoyed such praise from well-known and important people the world over, I began to accept that my ambitious dreams were likely to be in a pathetic class of non-happenings.

As the meeting was going on, my friend touched me and made a sign that I should look at the window glass next to me. The windows were closed. I saw a member of the security branch whom I knew. He did not seem to have seen me or my friend. He was concentrating on the speakers on the podium. We felt very uneasy because, as policemen, it would become an issue that we were attending a political gathering all the way from Mayville to Umlazi and at night. This also indicated to us that Prince Buthelezi was being monitored by the Security Branch. There was, at this meeting, the late Princess Magogo, the mother of Prince Buthelezi. The meeting carried on until late in the night with people enjoying the speeches and insisting that it go on, until the prince had to plead to the people that his mother was tired and had to be allowed to go and rest and that it would be unfair for the crowd to insist on her stay. It was then time for the next miracle I was anticipating, which would be at the end of the meeting when the prince went around the hall shaking hands with the people. I felt jittery because, with me, it was not going to be an ordinary hand shake but one that would send a message to say, 'I wish there was a chance we would meet under favourable circumstances for me to find out if you received our letter.'

The chance of such an opportunity never came. The unrest that followed some years later made it harder and harder for me to find out about the letter. The United Democratic Front and the Inkatha Freedom Party became adversaries in a bloody confrontation, which muddied relations between people and created distrust and hatred, leaving death and destruction in its wake.

Chapter 14
Joining the Detectives

It started with my love of writing. When I walked the beat at Mayville Police Station, when my police career had just begun, I developed an interest in writing into my pocket book in great detail. Others would only write, 'Time reported on duty and off duty.' They would note times between reaching and departing from regulation points on their beats. In between, there would be entries in their pocket books made by their supervisors who would write the time and point when they visited the member on the beat. The inspectors would also note such in their own pocket books.

I would write things like what had happened on parade when we were posted to our beats. I would note the kind of remarks made by the relief sergeant and responsive comments, if any, made by the members. I also made note of warnings and pieces of advice on alertness throughout our period on the beat. I simply enjoyed writing things. I always wrote down very clearly in my pocket book whatever I saw and did along my beat. At the end of our relief, we would hand over our pocket books to the charge office sergeant, who would check and file them.

It so happened that a charge office sergeant who inspected the pocket books in the charge office got interested in the manner in which I wrote entries into my pocket book. He reported to the station commander who called me in and, after a short interview, told me that he was transferring me to the Enquiries Department which dealt with motor accidents investigations and common assaults. We were two black constables and a young Afrikaans-speaking constable. We worked very well together and our standard of work was impressive, at least from what we heard from our superiors and members of the public we served.

Mayville Police Station was one of the newly built police stations around Durban. Most of the serious crimes in the Durban area were investigated from the station. The police cells were built in such a way that escape of prisoners awaiting trial would be very difficult. Prisoners known to be hardened criminals, or facing serious charges, were detained and interrogated from at the station by selected interrogators who assembled there every morning.

The detectives selected for those interrogations were special people. There was no murder and robbery unit covering Durban at that time. Whenever there was a serious crime in Durban or its suburbs needing special attention, well-known and specially gifted detectives would be drawn from other stations around Durban. This left Mayville Police Station to be used mainly for detention and interrogation of suspects. There used to be an array of white and black mastermind detectives in the assembled unit.

For some reason, the black detectives collectively took a liking for me and sometimes invited me to listen in when they interrogated their suspects. They also encouraged me to actually participate. When I asked suspects relevant questions, I observed, looking from the corner of my eye, how my seniors reacted. I saw them nod their heads in appreciation and exchange smiles of approval. Those were my mentors. I often stopped to wonder whether it was not part of a heavenly conspiracy to help me build my career by placing such exceptionally-gifted people at certain important stages of my life.

Remember what I said of some of the teachers who had taught me at school. They and these men seemed to be passing a baton in a relay race to clear my way to hit the top of victory somewhere in the distant future. Something told me, 'I am on my way.'

Those detectives taught me brilliant ideas in terms of dealing with suspects under interrogation. The most important thing I learnt from them was to create, however difficult, an environment of calm and ease between the suspect and the interrogators. Never threaten or fight or apply aggressive tactics to a suspect, they said. Suspects expect police officers to be hostile to them and they prepare themselves for it. When they come across calm, albeit firm and considerate detectives or interrogators, the suspects are disarmed of their own aggression and apprehension. The defence or denial they had prepared would be useless. They would then have to rehearse new denial tactics for which there would be no time. The long-term gain of that approach by the interrogator was that trials within trials in court were minimized. The question of whether a confession was induced through coercion or was voluntary was somewhat taken care of. The environment under which interrogations took place played an important role during court trials.

The other advantage, in the long-term, was that even if the accused were convicted in the end, trust was built between the policeman and the accused. Those prisoners had a tendency of spreading the word to others about the considerate behaviour of a detective. Later on, this would be shown as having produced wonderful results and success. The use of these tactics accounted for career boosts for the detectives who practiced them.

There would be other real-life encounters along this journey where unlikely characters got drawn together in an accidental, unintended alliance. This could result in embarking on acts of compassion to rescue one from difficult and complicated situations. This could evolve further, even though I never went out of my way to appeal for such help and compassion, except in prayer, the power of which I strongly believe. Those who recognize it the way I do will understand exactly what I mean. Those who do not are free to believe otherwise.

*****

It all started in 1963 when the detectives who interrogated suspects at Mayville Police Station invited me. One day, when I was busy helping with the questioning of a suspect under their careful attention, my acting Branch Commander at the time visited the interrogation area. It was one of the open, unused garages in the police yard. He was a grey-haired, past middle age, man. He smoked one of those bent tobacco pipes which he seemed to enjoy clearing and refilling with fresh tobacco from a shiny silver pouch. He seemed to have no regrets about the shape of the earth and how it impacted upon his day to day life. He spoke Zulu very fluently and with pride, not just with great feeling, but also for obvious enjoyment. His name was Detective Sergeant Buzuidenhoud.

He listened to me as I took part in the interrogation of a suspect with the special team of detectives. When he left to go to his office, he asked me to follow him, which I did. At the office, he asked me if I was interested in joining the Detective Branch. I was momentarily shocked with disbelief. The dream of becoming detective that I had held on to from the beginning of my police career was coming true, so unexpectedly and so soon. I said, "Yes sir". He then told me to sit down and write an application to join the Detective Branch.

He actually led me in writing the application. While I was writing he was typing his own recommendation, which he attached to my application and took it to the Headquarters. A few days later, he phoned the station from Headquarters to say that I must sort out my work at the enquiries section and report to his office the following morning to start as a probationer detective under him.

The following morning I reported to the sergeant in charge of the enquiries section and handed my dockets and case book to him. At the same time, I informed him that I was going away as of that morning to start my probation as a detective.

On reporting at the Detective Branch I was allocated a table in an office where I worked with two other detectives. Sergeant Buzuidenhoud stressed that he would be there for me and that I should ask whenever I was not sure of anything. He gave me an assignment pertaining to assault with intent to do grievous bodily harm. It involved a black man who had been assaulted under the Tollgate Bridge in Mayville and had been taken to hospital. He wrote a number of instructions in my diary and said that all that I had to do was to comply with those instructions; and if I did exactly as he had instructed I would have a successful investigation in as far as that case was concerned.

When I went to the hospital to see my complainant, I got the shock of my life to hear that he had died of the injuries he had sustained. I was shaken because this was my very first docket and, instead of a grievous assault, it had become a case of murder. I reported to the sergeant that the docket he gave me was now a murder. I pleaded with him to give the case to some of the senior detectives with me in the office. He said he would not take away the case from me because he still stood by what he had said to me about answering questions. My part was to comply with instructions he would write in my diary from time to time.

The man who died was unknown and his body was moved to hospital mortuary. The first instruction from the sergeant was that I go and take the deceased's fingerprints so as to establish his identity. I had never been to the government mortuary, let alone to obtain fingerprints from a dead person. Actually I had never touched a dead body. Nonetheless, I went to the government mortuary and found two old black policemen in attendance. They showed me the tray in which the particular deceased body was kept.

They helped place the body in the slab used for conducting post mortems. I then stood there not knowing what to do. Meanwhile, the two mortuary attendants were watching with a kind of amusement. One of them asked if I wanted help, I told him that it was my first time to enter a mortuary and I had never before had anything to do with a dead body and, moreover, I was just a probationer and that this was my very first case.

It was a very hot day. I felt I had to take off my jacket but could not see any place in the mortuary where I could put it. I started to sweat because of the heat and the fear in me. One of them then asked me to step outside. He pointed to a bottle store down the road, and said that if I walked to the store and bought them a bottle of wine they would help me with the fingerprints.

I did as instructed. I came back with the bottle of wine and I handed it over to one of them. Then, he gave me a shock of his own. He drew out a tray with another dead body placed the wine bottle against the frozen body and pushed the tray back. Then, both of them went about taking fingerprints from the body in my case. When they were through, and while I was packing the fingerprint forms in my briefcase, they washed their hands, fetched a glass and the bottle of wine from the closed tray with other body. They started drinking and thanked me for the wine. They were happy, it seemed, talking all the time as they continued to do their work and drink the wine.

Both looked like far gone alcoholics. Their faces and shaking hands told a story. I would later hear from other policemen that mortuary attendants were the only policemen allowed to drink on duty. I am not sure if it was true but that was a popular story about them and there were no dissenting voices about it.

When I left the mortuary those two guys told me that anytime I had a body whose fingerprints needed taking I knew the drill. I would have no problem once I complied.

Back at my station I told the Branch Commander who laughed when I told him about my fear at the mortuary. He said he did it deliberately and ensured that I went there alone because he knew that I would always get help from the two mortuary attendants.

The case was solved and went to court, and the accused was found guilty and convicted. The prosecutor in the case wrote a lengthy commendation about how well the case was investigated. When my branch commander saw that, he was overjoyed because he knew that the prosecutor who presented the case to the court had studied the whole of my docket and seen helpful instructions which he (the Branch Commander) had been writing to guide me in my diary. Complying with the instructions of the Branch Commander and the subsequent success of the investigation made me someone whom he felt committed to empower and impart the best of his experiences to. And thus, detective Sergeant Buizedenhoud became my first mentor as a detective.

Chapter 15

Making my First Impact at a New Station

In 1965, I was transferred to Hillcrest Police Station because a black detective constable working there was under criminal investigation for alleged extortion and fraud. He was sent to work in my place in Mayville until his case was heard in court.

At Hillcrest, Detective Warrant Officer Kleinhans - who was the branch commander - told me that I had been recommended to him by the Durban West District Headquarters as someone very capable. He wanted to test me by drawing out some old problematic cases which they had failed to solve, but which he felt could be solved based on what he had been told about me.

The case he drew was a two-year-old robbery from Assagay Road in Bothashill where a lot of clothes and a firearm had been stolen. There had been a suspect whom they had questioned but failed to get him to confess, although they had very strong suspicion against him.

When they brought him into my office, he squatted on the floor against the wall. They had fetched him from a farm where he worked as a labourer. I greeted him and asked him to sit on the chair next to the table in front of me. I also told him to relax because I was not going to fight with him, because it was not my habit to fight with suspects or witnesses. I told him that, according to the judges' rules, he was not obliged to say anything with regard to the allegations I was going to put to him, and that should he decide to say anything it would be used in court as evidence against him. I told him that I was under an obligation to warn him as I had just done. It appeared to me that he had never heard of what I had just told him. He appeared very confused and pleaded with me to repeat what I had said, which I willingly did.

I went on to explain to him that he was within his rights to remain silent if that was what he chose to do or get himself a lawyer to represent him when I asked him questions.

He breathed a sigh of relief. He calmly said that it was confusing to him that he was brought to a detective five years later for the same case yet it did not matter if he spoke or not. He thought seriously that there was a catch somewhere.

I explained to him that it was not a case of my not being bothered about whether he kept silent or spoke. I was not telling him to remain silent. I was merely carrying out the judge's rules, that I warn him because thereafter it would be his choice. I gave him the example that he had a right to deny the allegations put to him, and a right to an alibi, which he could seek to confirm his denial. It was for me the first time I had to explain what I meant by saying that a suspect had a right to remain silent. I knew that detectives had a problem with the judges' rules that said, they should warn the suspect at the time of arrest that he or she had a right to remain silent. I personally had been administering the contents of the judges' rules to the suspects I arrested but all I had received from suspects were denials, but never a suspect saying that he or she was opting to remain silent.

When I outlined the case to the suspect, and before he responded, I gave him a broad outlook of the dangers of being in possession of an unlicensed firearm, and also the temptations the presence of a firearm in his possession would offer whenever he was annoyed. Any other person having knowledge of his possession of a firearm would feel threatened and report him to the police or remove the threat by killing him. That firearm could also go rusty and rendered useless or dangerous after so many years of being badly kept and not cleaned. If it fell into the hands of other people who might use it and get caught, they would point him out and he would still face a case of its theft and use. I impressed upon him that, as long as that firearm was not in the hands of its rightful owners or in the hands of the police, he would never claim to be free and my purpose was to negotiate with him the process of his freedom. I pleaded with him to work with me towards that end.

After a long silence he breathed a big sigh as if he had been disarmed and responded by saying, "I understand exactly what you are saying but the problem I have is that you have no evidence about my involvement in the case but you are cleverly trying to trap me into helping you with evidence to convict me." He went on to say that if he helped me to convict him I would be the only one to benefit by it.

I told him that was not true because he benefited from the money and all the other valuables he took from the complainants' house and yet I was only asking him to hand over only the firearm which could lead him to trouble. I made it clear to him that I was not going to lie to him that he would not be charged or convicted. However, if he was cooperative, he would call me in court in his evidence in mitigation and I would under oath tell the court that it took less than twenty minutes after I had spoken to him in my office for him to produce the firearm and that he was of help in my investigation of the case.

I also told him I would tell the prosecutor that I would not be averse to a lenient sentence. He asked me if I had a cigarette. I asked for one from my colleagues and gave it to him. He took a few large drags, exhaled and watched the haze of blue smoke drift away from his nostrils like mini clouds. I stood up to stretch myself to afford him a little time to satisfy his craving. I handed him an ash tray and sat down again as I expected him to make an important announcement in response to all that I had said so far.

Indeed he threw down a surprise, saying, "Get a car and fill enough petrol to get us to Ndwedwe District." That was a distance of about fifty kilometres from Durban. I got two of my colleagues to accompany me. I reported to my branch commander that I was taking the suspect to Ndwedwe District.

We got to the suspect's home in the rural area of Mzinyathi and he asked for a spade from his people and he dug next to the cattle kraal, unearthed a plastic bag and handed it to me. There was, a .38 revolver in the bag with five bullets wrapped separately in a cloth. His relatives came to watch as he dug up the firearm and he explained to them not to worry because he had come to realize that it had to be taken back. He asked if I could wait while they prepared food for him. I told him that because curious people were beginning to gather around and were becoming interested, it would be better for us not to wait. I sensed it was becoming risky hanging around the place. His relatives gave him money and, on our way, he bought bread and milk from a local shop which he ate in the car. He also bought himself a packet of cigarettes and smoked as we drove on.

The importance of it all was that an offence he had committed five years earlier, for which he was detained and interrogated by detectives and later released because there was no evidence to charge him, was solved within an hour after I was asked to talk to him. The branch commander could not believe his eyes when he saw the firearm, which was also proven to be the one stolen in the case in question. As promised, I gave evidence in mitigation and he got a sentence lighter than he would otherwise have received. That case formed part of my being regarded as a specialist interrogator during my career as a detective.

Chapter 16
Poor, m, yet Arrogant and Demeaning

There were white Afrikaans-speaking men who were railway bus drivers along routes where black people commuted. They usually were fluent in black (Bantu) languages. Those who worked in Zulu, Xhosa, Sotho, Bapedi or Setswana speaking areas were fluent in those languages. I know one who drove a railway bus in Natal (KwaZulu Natal) and his bus travelled mostly in rural areas. He used to have a black male assistant who acted as a conductor, and saw to order in the bus by the black passengers.

The driver had no respect for his black passengers. In fact, he had such contempt for them. Indeed, it was saddening to see black men and women full in a bus, driven by a single white man, through large rural areas, far away from any places with whites, being so arrogant and abusive to them. It was as if he was sure that the colour of his skin was a guaranteed protection for him, wherever and whenever he may find himself in the midst of black people.

He was, and would always be the boss in the midst of blacks. He knew blacks had been intimidated enough to surrender whatever self-esteem or dignity they had. One shout would get the police on the scene, and they would not be there to serve them but to further demonstrate to them that their purpose was to ensure that blacks did, at all times, remember their place and never dare cause whites to doubt their superiority in the apartheid South Africa.

The most that he knew in the Zulu language was swear words of the nature that would cause a mini war if used by blacks to other blacks. However, in his case blacks just laughed and showed surprise and admiration of his deep knowledge of the Zulu language. It was a sickening experience to be in his bus enduring his demeaning arrogance and stupidity. That was also one of the kinds of trash black South Africans had to endure in apartheid South Africa.

Chapter 17
The Day I Saw Apartheid Kill a White Man

One time, I was standing in front of the Mayville Police Station watching the beautiful sun majestically easing itself beyond the Jan Smuts Highway. It left a golden glow which ignited a sense of hope and love for life. This was a welcome sight, especially at the end of a warm, cloudless and quiet day.

The peace of that moment was disturbed by the sight of a South African Railways bus which was zigzagging up the road leading towards the police station with screaming passengers. Half of them were hanging at the windows as if they wanted to throw themselves off the bus.

Before I could turn to alert the other policemen around at the charge office, it seemed that the other policemen had already noticed what was happening and were rushing to the road. When the police eventually stopped the bus, which was en route from Pietermaritzburg to Durban, most of the passengers were already on the road running towards the charge office. The bus was driven by a white, middle-aged Afrikaans-speaking man who appeared to be highly intoxicated. The passengers were all black and were mostly women. Some had been injured, having been knocked around when the bus was zigzagging on the road. The passengers who came into the charge office and in the yard were hysterical.

They were demanding that the driver of the bus be locked up because he nearly killed them. The white policemen took the driver to a little office behind the charge office. They (the white policemen) did not seem to be processing any papers to have him charged or examined by a doctor or district sergeant. There was a lot of noise in the charge office, with people demanding that their statements be taken as some got injured trying to jump off a moving bus because of the driver's drunken state and reckless driving. A white sergeant came into the charge office equally hysterical and shouted loudly, "Shut up all of you, and get out of my office or else I am going to lock all of you up for trespassing and disturbance".

The people shouted back and said they were complainants who had come to the station to report a case and the charge office sergeant had no right to chase them away or lock them up as if the station belonged to him. He instructed the black policemen to remove the people from the police station because they were, according to him, 'causing a disturbance'.

The black policemen started retreating from the crowds in order to avoid the white sergeant's unlawful instructions. They were also avoiding questions directed at them from the passengers, such as, "What are you black policemen here for?" "Why don't you arrest the drunk driver, because you have also seen that he is drunk?". "Why are you not willing to take our statements of complaint?" Black policemen felt exposed and ashamed that they could not help the passengers in any way when in fact they knew it was their duty to do so.

I did not move away and remained where I was until the sergeant came to me and asked if I did not hear when he gave the instruction that those bus passengers had to be removed from the charge office and the premises. I asked him, "How are you suggesting we remove them?" He asked me if I was defying a lawful instruction. I said to him, "Let us say I was agreeing to remove them and asking for guidance. The people did not want to move and they were at the station legally." I went on to say that I wanted to know how I was meant to find out whether he meant I had to push them, beat them up or shoot them. The crowd burst out laughing and some women started ululating in approval of my stand. One at the back of the crowd uttered a muffled shout of Africa. I decided to move away from the whole thing, which, for me, was becoming politically unhealthy. I could attract unnecessary attention from the politically alert white policemen. The one who was trying to engage me about removing the bus passengers was one of the dull and naive ones.

When the passengers from the bus realized that it was getting late and they had actually not been seriously injured, and that another driver would not be sent to replace the drunken one even if they had paid for the full journey, they decided to move from the station and continue on their journey on Indian buses. As soon as they had left and it was quiet, two white policemen escorted the drunk driver to his bus across the road. They helped him into the driver's seat, and he drove away. One of the white policemen who dealt with the driver whilst he was at the police station was saying that a white person could never be arrested on the demands of blacks. That should not happen anywhere in South Africa, he averred.

About fifteen minutes after the bus had continued, a police radio message came in stating that there had just been a major accident on Berea Road where a Railways bus crashed onto the rails and the driver was fatally injured.

The next morning there was a newspaper report blaming the Mayville police for allowing the driver to carry on when it was obvious that he was drunk. If that driver had been black, he would have been saved because he would have been stopped from driving the bus, arrested and charged. There was a bus load of witnesses to the drunken driving of the white bus driver who was released by the police. How ironic! The bus driver died because he was white and it was at the hands of the apartheid police.

Chapter 18
A Young White Police Detective's First Kill

Hatred directed at blacks by some naive whites in the police force was very entrenched at the time. Those who did not speak Afrikaans, but were eager to be seen to be loyal to apartheid, displayed extraordinary behaviours. They seemed eager to demonstrate their loyalty and enthusiasm to implement the ugliest elements of apartheid whenever a chance arose. When they tried to do that, they appeared quite blind to the existence of their black colleagues. They could do whatever they wanted to do, irrespective of how their actions would affect fellow black people, policemen and civilians. Those were the people who seemed to have been brought up with the notion that blacks were inferior people or non-humans and with no feelings.

In the mid-1980s, we received a report of a crime in operation. It was an armed robbery in the Dassenhoek area outside Pinetown. Available detectives and some uniformed policemen responded by rushing to the scene. There ensured a chase of the black suspect who was shot and killed by a young white detective. As far as that went, the shooting was justified in the eyes of those involved. The suspect was a known criminal and was in an armed robbery action at the time.

What became odd, and in fact macabre, is when the young white detective who had shot and killed the suspect, openly exhibited excitement, jumping like the proverbial headless chicken! As he did this most white policemen were congratulating him, as if he had saved the country from a certain catastrophe. Then he announced it was his first kill before phoning his parents to break the 'exciting' news to them.

What was disturbing to us black detectives about this kind of celebration, was not that a black suspect was shot, but the extent of jubilation demonstrated by white detectives who quickly arranged *braai* (barbeque) at the station, purely to celebrate the shooting of a black suspect. It left wondering and thinking what kind of a family would condone that kind of behaviour of their son in celebrating his killing of a person, especially in a matter with such racial overtones. I was alarmed at the young white detective's behaviour after the shooting and killing a suspect. I was not persuaded by the fact that he had shot a suspect, a black criminal, or that I was myself a kind of weakling who harboured a desire that all police operations should under all circumstances be silky smooth and as bloodless as the mountain snow.

I had personally been involved in ugly situations and did not underrate the brutality and the little regard for life by criminals who had nothing to lose. In their way of thinking they had plenty to gain by killing a policeman. Policemen stood in the way of their reign of terror of being feared and adored by those to whom they displayed their ill-gotten wealth and demonstrated how to spend it.

I was alarmed because that was my first close look at how young white minds were being destroyed by apartheid. These people were supposed to be Christians. When I was issued with my service pistol, the first thing I did was to pray to God for protection from any situation where, in the performance of my duty as a policeman, I would have to shoot and kill a person. I asked God to allow for no situation where I would be called to defend myself by shooting and killing anyone, let alone one in flight or unarmed. My prayer in this regard was answered in full. I retired from the police force after 33 years without having been called upon, by any manner of pressure or desire, to use my service pistol.

Chapter 19
A No-Win Situation

In the midst of the political upheaval in the schools for black kids in KwaZulu Natal and elsewhere, it so happened that I got into a situation which demanded extreme courage and swift thinking. Unrest was flaring up from school to school. Students from high schools and colleges were up in arms with school authorities over high school fees, bad food and unacceptable rules, according to the students. A kind of programme of un-governability was in action.

At the time, my wife was working at one of the teacher training colleges as a housemother, a matron. She occupied one of the staff quarters at the college. Her lounge and kitchen were on the ground floor, while the bedroom and bathroom were upstairs. One had to climb a flight of stairs to get there. There were girls' and boys' blocks and my wife's quarters were in the girls' block.

I was there one night when boys from the boys' block attacked the girls' block over some dispute they had earlier had. The boys were forcing themselves into the girls' block, beating some girls and trashing the place. They were opening taps and spraying the girls with water from hose pipes. It was clear that some of the boys were under the influence of alcohol and staggered along, causing mayhem in the volatile situation.

My car was parked close to the entrance of my wife's quarters. Some of the boys were leaning against the car and urinating on the side. The situation was such that if any of the invading boys noticed or identified my car, they would have raised an alarm and possibly shout, "Here is a policeman's car and he is inside the matron's quarters." I would have been targeted immediately for destruction. This would have been because of the then prevailing animosity between the comrades and the police. Before they would have got to my wife's bedroom upstairs, they would have had to climb up in a single file, given the nature of the stairs in the house. The prospects of being attacked became quite real. I felt that I had to avoid panicking, should that happen, and start thinking very fast on a more palatable way out!

The first thing I ruled out was the idea of shooting at them, as they would be climbing up the stairs in a row. I quietly reasoned that although I would have killed many, and most probably scared others away, it would not have been worth it. Why would I kill maybe ten young people, students for that matter, to save my single life and dignity? Would I have life and dignity without freedom? Would it make sense for me to kill those on a mission (if killing me, a policeman would serve that purpose) to free me and the lot of other black people just because I happened to have a gun and worked for the oppressors?

I imagined newspapers the following morning screaming, *Black policeman guns down ten student activists inside their campus!* The media would have wanted to add colour to their stories, saying, *South Africa's notorious black Security Branch policeman lines up ten students and shoots wild-west style.* I imagined my name being published as that of the perpetrator, who single-handedly massacred ten young people. I imagined a black ball of smoke descending upon my family, my friends and my community. I imagined those ten young people lined up before religious ministers, stunned teachers, with uncontrollably wailing and cursing parents. I imagined students in uniforms forming guards of honour, toy-toying comrades baying for my blood, my house and its contents already smouldering in flames. The ANC would be shocked beyond belief. They would be deemed to have not died in vain because the whole world would be shocked.

With these thoughts in my mind, I started sweating. I appealed to myself to consider other scenarios. If, with all these terrible thoughts, I decided not to prevent the students from getting to my wife's bedroom and finding me there, I would bravely ask them to listen to me before they did whatever they had intended. I went on to say, "I am not appealing to you not to kill me. I will only want you to make sure that I am the right target. I suggest we do it this way, while all of you wait here to guard me, I shall give two of you numbers to go and phone. Then tell the leaders who will answer that you have found me here, and you just wanted to make sure that you were doing the right thing by killing me. If those people say 'yes' then come back and kill me, if you feel that will hasten freedom."

I knew that if they had phoned, they would have been told to stop it. They would know the leaders whose names I would have given, and they would know me.

Then another scenario came crashing into my mind, raising my level of panic. What if I gave names of political leaders, thus revealing my association with them to comrades who were in fact police informers? What if they simply phoned their police handlers, and who, upon receiving such news, instructed their informers to tell the comrades that they had been given the green light to kill me, when in fact that was an instruction from their handlers?

This whole horrible debate in my head was almost maddening. Just then the noise of the boys' invasion into the girls' blocks subsided and they withdrew to their blocks, luckily, not with intervention of the police or anyone else. The whole thing ended as if I were waking up from a horrific dream.

Chapter 20
We were an Invisible Team

Our team came together around 1985 in Pinetown. We had been taken away from dockets and worked as a field unit. We occupied offices on the second floor of the new building on Old Main Road, and the floor was reserved for detectives. There were those who carried dockets in our unit and, in our unit, we have many experienced detectives. Security Branch detectives also occupied offices on the same floor.

Our unit was composed of members from Hillcrest, KwaDabeka, Westville and Pinetown. Sergeant Keswa, Constable Reggie Masango, Constable Zwane and I had all come from Hillcrest, constables Masango, Mhlongo and Zwane had been handpicked from the Uniform Branch to work in our field unit. Detective Keswa and I were full time detectives. From KwaDabeka came detective Sergeant Sibisi and detective Sergeant M. They were both accomplished detectives with experience in carrying dockets and investigating all kinds of cases. We had also found in Pinetown, detective Sergeant B. R. Thusi, Constable Msseleje and the late Sergeant Jrantse. All these members were specially selected because of their performance at their previous stations. There were a few white members on the team. I cannot recall who they were and where they had come from.

At first, Captain Breect was in charge of the unit. Lieutenant Frank Dutton, who was there at the time, took over later.

The team had a very good record in combating crime in the area it covered. This area consisted of the whole of the Durban West Police District, but concentrated especially around Hillcrest, Pinetown, New Germany, Westmead, Kloof and the surrounding rural areas of Molweni, KwaNgcolosi, Nyuswa and Ntshongweni. Those were extensive areas with a fair share of criminal activities. We also covered Kwa Dabeka and Clermont Townships.

The most prevalent crimes in the rural areas were faction fighting, robberies, rapes, thefts, murders, stock thefts, serious and common assault, attempted murder, and house breaking in the urban areas. We spent most of our time on these crimes. Our team really shone when it came to solving cases in the areas mentioned. Detective sergeants Sibisi Mothuli and Thusi were experienced and skilful.

The prominent characteristics of our unit involved avoiding rough tactics in dealing with suspects. We had intense training on the use of tactics, which excluded coercion to get confessions from suspects or cooperation from witnesses. We aimed at making sure that none of our members got accused of assaulting suspects for purposes of extracting information from them. Most of our cases had uncontested confessions in trials, and we won those that did surface. Our members were highly motivated and dedicated and team spirit was high. I think our good crime reduction record got the authorities to take note because they relied on our team to solve such complex matters as politically motivated violence. Soon, our unit was assigned such cases.

There was a white woman from a house which had been burgled and her property stolen. When a white policeman and I visited the scene, she behaved in a way which indicated to me that although I was there and as large as ever, she did not seem to notice me. It seemed like she did not recognize that she was talking to two policemen. Even as we walked into the house, she seemed uncomfortable, especially when I walked into the bedroom. She made all kinds of signals to indicate to the white constable that she would rather I did not enter the bedroom. I took note of that and just stayed back. Inwardly, I felt sad and sorry for her naivety, because I needed to know the details of the scene and what had been stolen in order to be able to help her. It appeared stupid of her to try and protect the sanctity of her bedroom when the burglars had already violated the place! To boot, they had entered without her permission.

When she walked out from the bedroom with my colleague, she was saying to the constable, "You know officer, as soon as I entered the house, I could immediately smell that the whole township was here". As she spoke, she turned to look my way but not at my face, perhaps to check for my reaction. I could also see that her conscience touched her a little bit, but she suppressed it with the thought that the white officer was in a way in agreement with her remark. This indicated that she was on the 'Hatred for Natives' campaign, of which she doubtlessly thought that the white policeman was part. She also would have perhaps felt that what she said in front of me was not bad after all, because I was also part of the township brigade and I must carry the message to my black thieving brothers out there.

The kind of attitude by the likes of that woman had grave implications. For example, for a white complainant to demonstrate her hatred for a black police man in front of a white policeman who, (the black policeman) would in all probability be the one to solve the case was bound to be counterproductive. The white policemen knew that they could only solve cases where black suspects were involved through help from the very same despised black policemen. Black policemen therefore found themselves having to think hard whether to help the whites who hated them or the black criminals who were hated together with them by the whites.

The front door incidence

I went to a house one morning on Vause Road in Durban. I was in full police uniform and had a warrant for the arrest of a black gardener who worked there. I got up on the veranda and knocked on the door. The owner of the house, an elderly white woman, opened the door. She appeared very annoyed and angrily enquired, "What do you want at the front door?"

I was puzzled as I was not expecting such a question. I could only say, "Good morning madam, I am from the police."

However, before I could finish, she butted in, "Do you think I can't see that?"

I found it difficult to be polite under the circumstances. I took out the warrant for the arrest of her gardener and I said that was my purpose for calling.

She read the warrant and when she looked at me, I said in a firm voice, "Where is he?"

She said, "But you can't come here and arrest him just like that".

I said "How do you suggest I arrest him when I have a warrant to arrest him? Those are instructions from the court".

She then started cooling down, directed me to a chair and asked me to wait there while she went to call him. I said she did not have to worry because, as indicated in the warrant, I also had to search for the weapon he had used on the victim he stabbed. She said "Why don't you just take him without seeking to make his position worse in the court by exhibiting the weapon there?"

I stood up and told her to stay out of the matter, and that I was going to the gardener's room to arrest him, search for the exhibit and take him and the weapon if found to the police station.

I apologized for having knocked on her front door and went to the servant's quarters.

At the servant's quarters I found the gardener and a blood stained dagger. She witnessed the arrest of her gardener and she also saw the blood stained dagger. She said she wanted to know what would happen to the gardener. I told her that I was going to detain him and take him to court the following day.

When I left with the gardener, instead of saying goodbye, I said, "Again madam, sorry for knocking on your front door". I don't know how she felt, but I felt good.

Later, when I got to think about it, there was no doubt in my mind that most white people were undeclared members of a campaign to denigrate blacks whenever and wherever they came into contact with them. It was not surprising that many of them seemed intent on keeping apace what appeared to be a white South Africans pastime, hating and hurting blacks.

Chapter 21
The Two Twits' Dilemma

It was during the mid-1960s when racism and white arrogance were at their peak in the country. One day in the course of my investigative duties as a detective, I called at the personnel office in McCord Hospital in Durban to enquire about a black man. The information I had and depended on was that his surname was Ndlovu, and he came from a rural area in the Ndwedwe District.

I was accustomed to working with such scant information many times and I had been successful in a fair number of cases, especially when it involved black people from the rural areas. I was advantaged by the fact that I knew the culture, and working with minimal information was my forte.

I was thirty-one years old at the time with six years' service in the South African Police Force. I was already being recognized as a promising detective by my seniors and superiors.

At the reception, I found a tiny and very pretty young white girl of about eighteen or twenty years in the reception office. Given her beauty, size and outward looks, one could easily associate her with innocence and even brilliance.

On my part, I was neither thin nor short by any means. On the contrary, I was on the heftier side. Those close to me associated me with respectability and refinement. On that day, my encounter with the white girl receptionist at McCord Hospital would left me broken and possibly shuttered, if I had had no taste of life as a black man under apartheid. She assailed my dignity, seemingly innocent and not being aware that I had any. It would be interesting to know what she grew up to be and where she ended up.

Perhaps I should dwell a little bit on the aspects of my overall appearance at that time.

Rightly or wrongly, my appearance led me to expect from her not respect, but to realize that I was a black man who did not look like a boy or a non-entity. I was wearing a tailor-made fawn checked Harris Tweed jacket and a pair of brown socks and matching shoes. I had on a white shirt and a brown tie.

There would have been an aura of affluence about me, had I not only been a native detective in the racist apartheid South African Police Force. Indeed, in the environment that existed, I had no right to look the way I did on that day.

I believe that my appearance, on that day, placed me outside the periphery of the down-trodden. My provocative outfit in the South African of that day reminded me of British Lords whose first choice were Harris Tweed jackets and matching caps, carrying ivory-handled walking sticks as they walked their great Danes through Hide Park every morning.

This is how the painful encounter went.

As soon as I entered the office and proceeded to her table, she looked at me as if I were something the cat had dragged into the room. She looked at me from the head to the feet as if to announce my unacceptability, likely as an intruder worth showing to the door.

She had an authoritative voice which felt misplaced coming from her small mouth and beautiful face. In fact, under other circumstances, her face would have looked innocent and untainted. She said, "Don't you know you have to knock before you enter, even if the door is open?"

"I am sorry," I said.

She then retorted sharply, "I wish you were."

I realized that I had entered hostile territory. I had to prepare to face the firing squad. I remembered the saying 'dynamite comes in small packages'.

I introduced myself by saying that I was a native (as if she did not see that) detective from Mayville and I was trying to trace a man by the surname of Ndlovu from an area in the Ndwedwe District and I had been told that he worked at that hospital.

Looking at me contemptuously, she asked, "Is that all?"

I said, "Yes."

Then she went on, "Give me three things, and then I can listen to you. First give me the identity number, second his full names and the department in which he works."

I told her that I had none of the things she had just mentioned, the reason being that I had never met the man to be able to have his identity number. Secondly, the people who told me about him were not his relatives and there was no way in which they could know his identity number and his first name. That was the only information they had. I had hoped I would be able to get his department from her or from him.

She repeated what I had been saying, "You have not got his identity number, you have not got his first name and you have not got the department where he works. How on earth do you expect us to find him? Do you know how many people work in this hospital?"

I said, "I thought if I could speak to only two Ndlovus in this hospital they will know which Ndlovus are from Ndwedwe. Once I get to know about those at the hospital, I would find the one I was looking for, adding, "I am hoping that the registers will indicate which area of Ndwedwe your Ndlovus come from."

She said, "You want me to leave my work and go through the registers for you?"

I said, "No, no, I thought if you could give me permission to go through the labour register I could do it myself."

She retorted, "It does not work that way. Without the identity, the full name of the person, plus his department number, I cannot help you. I do not think you are serious, to think you can just walk in here and go through my registers as if you are an inspector Gee Wiz". She sneered and went on to say, "Look I have had enough of your gimmicks for the day and I think it is time for you to leave." She said this, indicating the door with her small head.

I then said that the last thing she could help me with was to show me the manager's office.

As if shaken by an electric shock, she jumped to her feet and said, "What is this? First you come here without a shred of information expecting me to find a worker with only his surname, and now you want to see the manager, what for?"

I was getting worked up too and ready to stand up to her and actually show her that I was not the mickey mouse policeman she was making me out to be. I said, "I will tell the manager what I wanted to see him for."

She picked up the phone, dialled, waited a little bit, and said, "Sir there is a man here who says he is a detective and is looking for one of our boys, and the only thing he has is the surname and nothing else. No first name, no identity number and no department." She then listened and said, "Well sir, you know how scrappy they are, and now he wants to see you." Then, "Yes sir, I will tell him." She turned to me and said, "The manager is coming."

Three minutes later, a tall white man in a white shirt and tie came down the steps and confronted me with the question, "What is your problem?"

I told him what I had told the clerk, where upon he said, "It is impossible to find a boy here without an identity number, worst still without full names. As a native policeman you should know that there would be hundreds of natives with one surname."

I said, "Thank you, sir" and turned towards the door.

When I reached the doorway the man in a loud voice asked, "What has the boy done anyway?"

When I said, "Nothing" he apparently became angrier and asked sharply, "What sort of a joke is this? We are sweating here trying to find a mysterious boy for you and you tell us that he has done nothing?"

I replied, almost stepping out, of the door, "The man I am looking for, according to my information, may be in a position to help identify a suspect implicated in a case where an old European woman was attacked and robbed in her house."

He held his hands above his head and exclaimed, "O my God, why did you not say this from the beginning?"

The clerk was also on her feet shouting her own "O my God, Oh! my God."

I walked out of the door and headed down the road towards the bus stop.

The man showed up at the door almost as if to follow me and shouted saying, "You cannot turn your back on me like that. I can report you to your superiors for this you know."

I continued walking and when I reached the main road and the bus stop, luckily the bus came right then and I boarded.

The clerk and the manager had not bothered to ask for my name. Although I had first mentioned my police station, the clerk had apparently not been listening. They had spent their time focusing on trying to denigrate and showing me as a clueless detective. I left them to stew in their stupor.

Chapter 22
Black Policemen Helping White Racists

This was not an ordinary case. It seemed to have all the hallmarks of an ugly statement.

One evening in Hillcrest, an obviously rich woman had a visitor, whom she had to see out. They proceeded to the guest's car who then left.

When the host returned to the house, she was suddenly accosted by unknown black males who apparently had been hiding in the dark somewhere on the premises.

She was ordered into the house and into her bedroom. They proceeded to order her to undress. They also saw her daughter in the house, and when they showed an interest in her as well, the mother pleaded with them to leave the daughter alone. She asked them to take whatever they wanted, if that would save her daughter. She even offered herself to be raped instead of her daughter, whom she claimed was still a virgin. They reminded her that they were in charge and needed no input from her on whatever they decided to do. They told her that everything would be fine as long as her daughter and she did not give them reasons to kill them.

The intruders were the lowest of low lives. They had emerged from the bush over the fence. No one knew how long it had been since they had had a bath or change of clothes.

One of the intruders, who appeared to be in charge, ordered two of them to start raping the madam, while he and the other one started with her daughter. They were going to take turns, after which they would move to the madam, while the other two would switch to the daughter.

One could not imagine the vile nature and deep-seated disregard of the dignity of any human being in the acts of these vile men. Whoever they were, and whatever they had done, the victims did not deserve anything like this. Indeed, no one deserved that level of animalistic behaviour and barbarism.

After the rape, the intruders ransacked the house and loaded whatever valuables they could lay their hands on into the owner's car and drove away. They left the madam and her daughter devastated and hateful.

I happened to be one of the detectives who visited the crime scene early the following morning. There had been other detectives and police who had been there that evening after the crime. It was an ugly and a very cruel crime that had visited that unfortunate family.

We searched for clues inside and outside the house. One of the black detectives found a button in the passageway and kept it for discussion among us. It was not identified as belonging to any of the members of the household. Others searched the servants' quarters. There were many servants. Some worked only in the kitchen, some cleaned the house, some did washing and ironing and others worked in the garden.

As we were busy interviewing those who worked inside the house, we noticed something very unusual with the behaviour of the housemaids. Each time we interviewed them, they would keep glancing at their watches with some agitation, seemingly very careful not to miss the time. We were concerned with that behaviour and started questioning one of the maids with a view to getting direct answers from her about it.

It had not ended with the frequent glances at their watches. It had gone as far as the servants asking that we let them go to their quarters for a while and then they would make themselves available for the continuation of the interviews. What was also strikingly noticeable is that they would return, having changed into fresh clothes.

It took moments of silence and apparent deep thinking for one of the maids to finally take a plunge into the unknown waters of what could be suicidal for her future as an employee of that household. We held our breaths, not knowing what bombshell awaited us as she seemed set on letting the proverbial cat out of the bag. She gathered herself together calmly and calculatingly unburdened herself of a dark secret. "We work for the most racist employers. They are an English-speaking family, but they are worse than any Afrikaans-speaking racist farmer. They hate black people more than anything else. As far as the madam is concerned, blacks stink. That is why those of us who work in the house have to have a bath, powder ourselves and change into fresh clothes four times a day." She continued, "As you see us dash from the house to our quarters and keep looking at our watches, we dare not miss our time to wash and change. The madam cannot tolerate black people," she said. She emphasized that she was saying this because we were all black. She would not have ventured into the subject if we had white detectives with us. The white detectives were all the while busy with the madam and her daughter and other whites who happened to be around.

What the maid said gave us a lot of food for thought. We were all labouring under the yoke of apartheid and knew that some of our white colleagues were unmitigated and irredeemable racists. We were directly affected, just as the servants were. She had an idea as to what had happened, and in fact, as to who could have done it. A maid had just been fired and, allegedly, not been paid. The sacked maid been very angry when she left. It was then suspected that she had sent the suspects to commit vengeful act.

After listening to the maid's story, we were very disturbed. Here was a very serious crime where a woman and her daughter were gang-raped in their house, their expensive car and household items stolen, and we had received the kind of information that would lead to the solving of the case. We had heard about extreme racism and slavery that was practised with black workers there. Some of us felt that the information about the madam's treatment of her servants killed the detective spirit in us.

There was a feeling that, because there were many white detectives at the scene, they had to prove themselves to the racist woman. They had to prove that they were better detectives by solving the case. There were also feelings that the intruders had taught the racists a lesson. The two women were raped by suspects who had come from a bush, without having washed for days. Then there was the prospect of one or all of the suspects being HIV positive. This would be a real tragedy for the family. There was also the question of reporting the information we had gathered to the white detectives.

We had to think carefully about the situation because, for such cases, racist white detectives had the habit of suggesting that the suspects had better be killed at the scene of arrest, or at any given opportunity.

That was not our thinking. We felt that if we arrested the suspects, we would have them tried in court. We felt that if we gave the information to the white detectives as our superiors, they would force us to reveal everything. This would result in the suspects being arrested under circumstances where we would not be able to protect them from being killed.

We would never condone crime. This one was committed with great cruelty, despite what we were told about the complainant being an extreme racist and black-hater. We were not detracted from our resolve to do the best we could to solve the case and get the culprits before a court of law.

By the end of that day we had had a breakthrough. Someone told us that he had seen the suspects enter a laundry in Pinetown. When we got there, we found some people had brought in clothing with blood stains. When we checked the clothing we found that one of the shirts had a centre button missing, and it was identical to the one we had found at the complainant's house. There was an address and a name on the copy of slip on the register in the laundry.

We worked until almost midnight trying to follow the clues. Someone led us to Pietermaritzburg where, according to our information, one of the suspects belonged. When we were about to leave to Pietermaritzburg, some of our white colleagues had had enough for the day and declined to proceed any further. They retired for the day and went to sleep. Several black and about two white detectives went along to Pietermaritzburg. We arrested some of the suspects there and discovered some of the property that was removed from the complainants' house on the night of the rape. The following day, the complainants' car was found in the Inanda area of Hillcrest.

When the interviews were taking place the morning after the rape, our white colleagues interviewed the complainant in the house while we spoke to black house maids and the gardeners outside. While the complainant had her hopes pinned on the white detectives solving her case, they had made little headway. This was a big case involving their own. It was one of the white warrant officer detectives in charge of the docket who was to give evidence. Because I had also played a lead role in collecting most of the important information on the matter, assisted by my black colleagues, I had to make a statement of arrest and recovery of some of the exhibits. I was required to give evidence for the state in the Supreme Court when the accused were prosecuted. It was then that it became clear to all who were present in court as to how the case was solved.

I received a special commendation from the trial judge for that. When the letter from the judge was written and sent to my headquarters by the prosecutor, he added his own concurrence to what the judge had said. He went further to mention the view of the courts in cases I had handled in the Supreme Court where he had presented state evidence. I wondered if the complainant, who was such a racist as alleged by her black staff, would appreciate that in the main, her case was solved because of the important input by black detectives.

Chapter 23
The Laundry Thief

I realized that patience and calmness were invaluable in successful crime detection. It was very important to be calm always, even in the face of antagonistic behaviour from a suspect under interrogation. Some suspects were intelligent and also experienced in their game. They would also study the behaviour of the detective conducting the interrogation and adjust their responses accordingly, knowing when to soften up or antagonize the detective. Some were accomplished actors who, through their made-up stories, would convince the detective of their innocence. They would also know when to detract the detective and break him or her from the momentum that would break the suspect's resistance and denial stance.

There was a laundry for dry cleaning about a kilometre away from the Mayville Police Station. Here a young black man left his pair of trousers for cleaning with the understanding that it would be ready for him to collect after work. There was a window which served as a counter where items for cleaning were received by laundry staff and picked up by customers when ready. One would ring the bell and service would be provided.

In the evening of the material day when the black man returned from work and got to the laundry counter, he found a brown paper parcel in the shape the black man was convinced was a pair of trousers. There was no one at the counter at that time. It was almost closing time and the person who was supposed to attend to him was busy inside the laundry. For some reason the black man decided not to ring the bell for service and just took the parcel and went away.

The following day he returned to the laundry and was arrested by the police when he was at the counter. The laundry belonged to an Indian family and both policemen were Indians. They accused him of stealing a pair of trousers belonging to an Indian man. He was later brought to me for interrogation.

I informed him of the allegations that he had stolen a pair of trousers belonging to someone else at the laundry. He denied, emphatically, that he had not found any trousers at the counter. He claimed that when he did not find his parcel as expected at the counter, because he did not find anyone there and had not been aware of the bell, he decided to leave.

He then planned to return the following day, a Saturday, to pick up his trousers as he would not be working. On Saturday when he called at the counter he was arrested.

The laundry worker, in his statement, said that he wrapped up a pair of trousers belonging to an Indian customer and placed it at the window counter. The usual procedure would have been that, when the customer came and found his parcel there, he would ring the bell for service. He would identify the clothing, pay for the service, get a receipt and leave.

In this instance, when the bell rang and when he went to the counter, he found the Indian customer complaining that his parcel was not there. The police were called and he gave a statement to that effect.

When all this was put to the suspect, he started crying bitterly, adding that he was a victim of racism because he was black. He directed his laments at me, claiming that of all people he would never have expected me to gang up against him when he knew that I was, like him, a victim of that kind of racism. He went asked why I could not see that the laundry in question belonged to Indian people, the pair of trousers allegedly missing was said to belong to an Indian person and he was arrested by policemen of Indian descent. "They may not have found an Indian detective to complete the whole conspiracy," he said.

During this session of weeping and ranting, he cursed the day he was born, and the fact he was born black. He said that he was sorry for me because it was clear to him that I did not know the Indians; that I was so naïve as not to see that the whole case was about the fact that they stole his pair of trousers and influenced the Indian customer to claim that he did not find his pair of trousers, when in fact he had found them. He felt that he had done enough to convince me that he was an innocent victim of conspiracy and that, indeed, if I were an African patriot I would have long offered him a shoulder to cry on.

As I said before, calm, patience, and sometimes nerves of steel defined a detective's worth. I had heard all the convincing denials from my suspect, one of which was, "Why would I have returned to the shop if I had taken my trousers without paying because there was nobody at the counter?" He told me that he had gone to his girlfriend's place of employment, where he had stayed with her in the servants' quarters where she stayed. I suggested to him that we go there and have a look. He seemed very willing. He even added that that was a good idea, because his innocence would be proven. He suggested that I was indeed also working in his interests, because there was no better way to prove his innocence than to search his room.

When we got to his girlfriend's place of employment, I approached her. She was with her employers in the kitchen, while another detective stood with the suspect in front of the servants' quarters. I asked his girlfriend what had happened to the trousers her boyfriend had brought home the previous night. Also, if it was in her room, I wanted to see it. She said that the trousers were no longer in her room, because when her boyfriend realized that they were not his and they did not fit him, he decided to take them back to the laundry. I went up to him with her and asked her to repeat what she had told me. She started by saying, "Is there a problem with the trousers, are they refusing to take theirs back and return yours?"

He responded by asking to talk to me privately.

I stood aside with him as he asked his girlfriend to go back into the kitchen as we entered the room where they had stayed the previous night. He started crying again and said he was crying because of all the things he had said to my face.

I told him that forgetting and forgiving was part of what constituted my being. He smiled and said I should relax because the matter had been solved.

He said that he took the parcel, thinking that it was his pair of trousers which he had left there for dry cleaning in the morning. The only mistake he made was that he took it without paying for it, thinking he would do so the following day. When he got home, he realized that the pair of trousers was not his and did not fit him. He told his girlfriend that he would take the trousers back the following day, Saturday. He took them along in the morning, and when he got close to the laundry, he hid them in some bushes and decided to go to the laundry to see if he was not being suspected of stealing. When he saw that he was not suspected, he would have surprised them by telling them what had happened and handed the trousers over. Unfortunately, he could not do that, because as soon as the Indians saw him, they called the police who came and arrested him. I accompanied him to the spot in the bush where he picked up the parcel containing the trousers, which the complainant identified as his.

PART 3
Skill & Honour

Chapter 24
How I Earned Trust from Criminals

I had a way of building trust between some criminals and myself. Those were criminals I had arrested and sent to jail, but while they were on bail or serving their sentences in prison, they valued the way I had treated them. I won their confidence so that sometimes when I happened to deal with difficult cases, I contacted them and sought their advice, which they freely gave. Prisoners, whom I had sent to serve sentences for their crimes, formed the most useful informer network during the whole of my detective career. I had a broad network of trusted, intelligent and loyal informers all over. They had been carefully hand-picked and none were ever exposed through carelessness on their part or mine. It broke my heart when I had to go on pension because I could not hand them over to other people. There was no provision, in law, to claim pension money for them, or say anything in private or public about their wonderful service, because of the secrecy around the nature of our relations and activities.

Here is an example of how that kind of prisoner/detective working relationship and loyalties operated.

A love-smitten Hollander, over sixty years old, whom I shall name Rostoff, worked at a factory in Westmead near Pinetown. He took his girlfriend, a curvaceous, beautiful, black girl, who worked with him at the same factory, for a lunchtime romance at what was known as a lovers' paradise on a hilltop in Marianridge. There were criss-crossing tarred roads, but no buildings or houses yet. Apartheid government's Immorality Act laws, which prevented love across the colour line, were very much alive at that time. This lovers' paradise, which was also a death trap, was the most 'tell-no-tales' convenience place for those whose houses or hotels were off-limit areas for illicit lovers.

Rostoff and his girlfriend drove along the tarred windings until they reached the top spot for their midday romance. Just when they started kissing, there was a shocking and a menacing knock on the window on the driver's side. When Rostoff looked, he saw a tall black man, dressed in a security guard's uniform, with a gun pointed at him. He was being ordered out of the car. As such, he opened the door and got out. As he did so, he noticed that there was a short black man armed with a large dagger which he held above his girlfriend, who was also ordered out of the car. The one posing as a security guard searched his pockets, took $4000 and R200 from him, and ordered him back into the car. They then ordered him to drive and leave the girl behind with them. He felt there was nothing he could do, seeing that these people were obviously dangerous criminals who were also armed.

As he drove down the windings towards the main road, he heard frantic screams from the direction where he had left his girlfriend with the two strangers. He realized that she was in serious trouble. He drove to Pinetown Police Station and reported the matter. He accompanied the police to the spot where he had left his girlfriend, only to find her sprawled on the ground with thirty-six stab wounds on her body. She was already dead, and the criminals were nowhere to be seen!

The case was booked to me for investigation. It was a brutal murder, committed by merciless, hardened criminals. I visited the scene and did my preliminary investigations.

Some three days thereafter, I was in the office very early in the morning, having worked through the night. I saw Mkebezo walking past our offices. He was coming from the charge office to report in accordance with his bail condition for the case of shop breaking and theft, and also for theft of a motor vehicle for which I had arrested him for about two weeks earlier.

I had also arrested him about three years earlier for suspected theft of heavy batteries, which I had been informed he sold to people for whom he provided electricity for their shacks in Dassenhoek location. I established that he stole the batteries from earth moving caterpillars and heavy road trucks from a site which was being cleared for a major building construction. That had taken place about three years earlier. I could not trace the owners of the batteries and he had to be released.

When I arrested him, he was staying with a friend of his in his shack. Before I released him, he had told me about a gang of robbers with whom he sometimes operated. He promised that he would give me information about their activities.

He disappeared for a long time thereafter until I received a case where a furniture shop had been broken into and a TV set and a number of radios stolen. A safe inside the office was broken into and cash to the value of six thousand Rand stolen. The thief also broke into an auto spares shop next door and stole a van with which he carried away the goods from the furniture shop.

While I was busy with the investigation of the case, I established that a shop owner had bought a van from a thief and when I followed up, found that it was the van that has been stolen from the auto spares shop. I later arrested Mkebezo and recovered most of the goods from the furniture shop and about three thousand rand of the money he had stolen from the furniture shop. Some of the money had been burnt when he used an angle grinder to open the safe. I allowed him bail of three hundred rand (R300) on condition he reported at Pinetown Police Station daily, between six in the morning and six in the evening.

It was during one of his reporting times that I saw him walk past the office and called him in.

We got into my office and I told him about the murder of the woman in Marianridge. He stood up and extended his hand to shake mine. As I hesitated, he said, "You know, now I believe when people say there is something you use for solving your cases".

I asked him what he was talking about. He said that in the criminal world, there was a popular belief that I used "muthi", or some form of black magic, to solve my cases. He then went on to say that he could now add his own audience to that, because he had seen it himself. I asked him to relieve me from my guessing and just tell me what he was saying.

He said, "I am saying now, your case has been solved." He went on to say that one day he went to the hills in Marianridge with his girlfriend and he stopped under a tree where there was nice shade. He and his girlfriend went to sit under the shade and soon thereafter a tall man wearing a security guard's uniform and a short one, wearing garage overalls, were standing on each side of them.

The tall one had what appeared to be a gun in his right hand, while the short one had a large dagger. The tall one even had a holster on his waist. When he looked at the short one, he recognized him. He said he decided to be sturdy and show no panic or fear, because he realized that these were criminals, and he, having been a criminal and a jailbird, knew how to handle them. He continued that he looked at the short one and said, "So this is the line you have now taken. Are you winning in this game?" He said the reply from the short guy was, "Yes indeed". He said, he then told them, "Gentlemen, I must leave you to it." Then he collected his rug from the grass and left with his girlfriend.

He then dropped his 'bombshell'. By asking, "Do you remember the night some three years ago when you arrested me for suspected batteries theft?"

I said, "Yes". He then said, "The short man with me in the room is the one who operates with the tall, supposed security guard." He gladly said, "Find your short guy and your case is solved". He gave me the name of the short guy as Mapawu. He did not know the tall guy's name. He thought he might have come from jail, as he could tell that the person was an experienced, old criminal.

At about ten o'clock that morning, I arrested the two suspects and recovered a lot of gold chains, rings, necklaces, bangles and many other items stolen from people who had gone to the 'love hill' and got robbed. I found the security guard's uniform in the tall guy's room, together with a toy pistol, and its holster. In the short guy's room, I found the garage worker's uniform jacket hidden under his bed and a blood-stained dagger, which later matched the blood of the deceased woman. He said they killed the girl because she recognized him and that the tall guy decided that she had to be killed. They had robbed a lot of Indian couples in Chartworth, at the spots frequented by lovers. Both of them were tried, convicted and sentenced to death.

In the meantime, Mkebezo got convicted to six years for his own troubles - the shop breaking and the theft of the van at auto spares.

After the conviction of the two murderers, I submitted an informer's claim for Mkebezo. When his money arrived I took it to him at Piet Retief Prison. With the help of prison authorities, the money was banked in Piet Retief.

A week after I got home, I received a letter from Mkebezo. He thanked me for being trustworthy, for having surprised him with the payment and reward for his services. He told me of a crime which had been committed by a gang in Marlvern. Robbers whom he knew waited for the house owner who had gone to fetch her children from school and when she returned and entered the premises, the robbers pounced on her, forced her and the children into the toilet, locked them there, ransacked the house, loaded their goods into the owner's car in which she had just arrived, and drove away. Following up on that information, I found that it was accurate, and it led to a big recovery of property, and an arrest was made. Later on, other prisoners introduced me to others in other prisons, even as far away as Johannesburg.

Most of the prisoners to whom I had been introduced were willing to volunteer information about other criminals who were still active outside. I capitalised well on my prison informer networks. Some of them called from prisons to say that I should ask the authorities to transfer them to Durban, so that they could point out certain criminals whom they knew had committed serious crimes. Just when I thought of seriously entertaining what these prisoners were suggesting, the prison authorities showed records of the same and warned me that those were escapers and were planning to escape on the way, as their records showed. It also turned out that when I tried to verify some of the information they had given me, I found it to be false. I ended up also broadening my knowledge about prisons and convicts.

Chapter 25
Respect and Recognition

Throughout my career, I made it a point to give my all when it came to performing my duties as a police officer. There were no half measures and no half-hearted commitments. I simply loved my work. I enjoyed the respect and recognition I was accorded as a result of my achievements.

There were times, however, when some of my efforts forced those who had been fed wrong and damaging information to distrust me. There was an ongoing suspicion that I was not to be completely trusted because some thought that my loyalties were divided between the ANC and the government. Some white officers told me so in my face, while others did the same behind my back. Those who thought that I was misunderstood reported it to me.

I served all those who depended on my service equally well. What puzzled some people was how I managed to earn respect from white policemen and white civilians who were regarded as loyalists to the apartheid government and its ideology. I was happy to have served them as well as I did. This made them doubt the negative things that they sometimes heard from their suspicious friends on the far right. Some even came to a point where they disbelieved anything negative said about me. It was good that they admitted this to me. I attributed their confessions to my impartiality when dealing with people of different races and persuasions. I did not hate those who did not agree with me because I knew that, if it was because of my race or my beliefs, it was a futile effort. I firmly believed that change was bound to come.

Of all the political organizations that operated in the country, I favoured the ANC. I thought The Freedom Charter[1] had all that was worth embracing and defending. Because my life revolved around fairness and truthfulness, whenever the games of politics in the country seemed intent on destroying the ANC, I had to do something.

The apartheid government had embarked on systematic persecution, which, among other things, included the elimination of certain individuals and groups within the ANC. As a policeman, I

---

1 **Editor's Note:** *The Freedom Charter was document published in 1955 by the African National Congress (ANC) and her allies and contained statements of democratic principles to govern South Africa that would apply in equal measure to all people regardless of race, language or religion.*

had to watch my steps when making any move. I felt that, in order to pursue my service to the people according to my calling and conscience, I could do something to positively impact outcomes. The only action I could take, in the strictest of secrecy, was to warn those of the ANC and other liberation movements through leaked information that harm was being planned against them in the form of death, arrest or some other such things.

I knew that apartheid was a fraud and a crime. As such I felt no guilt or had any qualms about acting against it in the manner I sometimes did. I am happy and proud because that did not affect my honesty and resolve in the pursuit of justice for all. Documented evidence in this regard adorns the prized shelves with my personal files.

PART 4
Intrigues and Woes

Chapter 26
UDF & IFP[1] Wars in Pietermaritzburg

In 1987, every news bulletin on South African radio and television would report on the number of deaths due to what was famously called black-on-black violence in KwaZulu-Natal. I became part of a specially selected team of detectives from Pinetown to investigate the murders, arsons, rapes and displacements that were the order of the day.

We assembled at Plessislaer Police Station and were provided accommodation in the police flats adjacent to the station. After we had settled in, we were prepared to begin the investigations. The following morning we were summoned to the yard outside where we found three brigadiers waiting for us. Standing next to them was a very thin, short, black man.

We stood at attention and listened to the brigadiers. They were all white and very senior in police ranks. One of them addressed us and said:

"I am not going to beat about the bush and I want you people to listen carefully. This team has been put together for the sole purpose of returning Inkatha people who have been chased away from their homes by the comrades (young men of the UDF). There is nothing else we have come to do here. One other thing, the leaders of the UDF in this area are the cause of the deaths that take place here on a daily basis and they are also the cause of the Inkatha people being forced to flee their homes. Some of them get raped and killed. Houses get looted and set on fire."

He went on to say,

"You people should understand, we have no interest in arresting the UDF leaders. We want them dead. Therefore do not hesitate to shoot them dead when you find them. To find out who they are, Sichiza here (indicating the thin black man next to them) has the list of them."

He then ordered Sichiza to step forward and read the list. The

---

1 **Editor's Note:** *The United Democratic Front (UDF) was founded in 1983 in South Africa and incorporated a number of anti-apartheid organizations at a time when mainstream anti-apartheid parties like the ANC were banned. On the other hand, the Inkatha Freedom Party (IFP) was founded in 1990 by Chief Mangosuthu Buthelezi and drew membership mainly from among the Zulu while using the Zulu cultural tenets as its foundation.*

names read out were those of Archie Gumede, Chairperson of the UDF in KwaZulu-Natal; A. S Chetty, a trade union member in Pietermaritzburg; Rev Africander of Pietermaritzburg; Sikhumbuzo Ngwenya of Pietermaritzburg and others whose names I cannot recall.

The brigadier sought assurance from us that we had heard him clearly, and we responded, "Yes Sir!".

The other brigadier wanted to hear from us as to whether we were all members of Inkatha. None responded and there was dead silence and tension.

The third one said it could not be good if our group consisted of Inkatha members. Still there was no response from us. As I was the senior most among the black members, he directed a question to me: "Who are you? Who do you support, the UDF or Inkatha?"

My response was, "We are here because two organizations are killing each other, the reason being that anyone who declares to belong to either of these organizations gets killed. We therefore feel that declaring who we are is unsafe. Let us be just policemen and be safe and do our duty.

At this stage it became apparent that pursuing the discussion on those lines was unhealthy, so it was abandoned. We were given the list and the officers left.

I felt very annoyed, helpless and trapped. I went to my room and tried to think of what to do given the circumstances we faced. I felt that it was best to resign from the police force because I had never had occasion to have it spelt out so clearly that police killed people.

For me, getting such instructions from three senior brigadiers was the last straw. I was not going to change from a policeman who always stood for justice and fairness, which I had done for more than 30 years, to one who would not only condone murder, but also kill people because of their political beliefs.

I took one of the detective vans we were using and drove straight to Clermont in Durban, hoping to see Mr. Archie Gumede. I intended to warn him of the impending action. As I drove around in his neighbourhood, I saw one of the vans from our camp in Pietermaritzburg. I was later to learn it was there for someone to point out Mr. Gumede's house to some of those in our group who had bought into the order to kill. I tried my best to warn the people, but also noticed that the killer brigade in our midst was watching me.

I thought seriously about the idea of resignation. Later, those of us who were not for the idea had a meeting. We resolved that should anyone in our group kill UDF suspects instead of arresting them, we would arrest the member and see if the brigadiers would interfere. We were preparing for the worst and resolved that if the authorities did not kill us, we would go to the press to expose their plans.

There were a lot of killings perpetuated both by Inkatha and the UDF. Most of the headmen and Amakhosi (chiefs) supported Inkatha, together with businessmen in the areas surrounding Pietermaritzburg. The townships were dominated by the comrades of the UDF.

At some time during the mayhem, followers of Inkatha attacked an old man Inkosi Zondi who belonged to a trade union. He had applied for a court injunction to stop the attacks on his homestead and himself. There were also threats to his life. The injunction against Inkatha was granted. However, his Inkatha enemies continued to attack until they killed him one day.

Our team arrested the perpetrators, took them to court, and they were convicted. The presiding judge commended us for that investigation. Nobody tried to stop us or interfere with the investigations.

One evening we were told to get ready to proceed to Mpumalanga Township in Hammarsdale to raid UDF comrades who were allegedly involved in the violence between the two parties. It was said there was information as to where they would be found. We got ready and waited. Late in the night, though, we were told that the raid had been cancelled and that we should wait for further notice.

In the morning we were told to go to Hammarsdale Police Station where we would get further instructions. At the station, we found a lot of comrades had been detained and some were under guard. Most of them had sustained injuries and we were informed that they were our suspects – the ones we were supposed to bring from Mpumalanga the previous night. The strange part of the whole thing was that, while they were supposed to be suspects, there were no complainants against them and there was no explanation as to where they were arrested and who had injured them or caused them to appear the way they were. There were no statements of arrest either.

We were instructed to take the suspects to our offices in Pietermaritzburg to be dealt with further by our team. Vans were provided and they were taken to our office to be fingerprinted and charged. They were about twenty or more.

When we started questioning them, we discovered that they had gathered in Unit One in the township. As comrades, during that time, they used to stick together in good numbers to protect themselves in case of an attack by their enemies. They said that on the night of their arrest the house where they were congregating was attacked by several white men and the Caprivi-trained Inkatha hit squad. They were then arrested and taken to Hammarsdale Police Station. No one came up with any particular offence that they were supposed to have collectively or individually committed.

I was the one who interviewed them individually in the office I was using. They stood in a long line and came in one by one to tell me what had happened and what they knew about the violent unrest in Mpumalanga Township.

What appeared to have happened was that the raid that was spoken about to us the previous evening was a planned attack on a UDF house by the police. It fell in line with what the three brigadiers had told us about killing UDF leaders when we arrived in Pietermaritzburg.

After I spoke to the suspects, I would pass them on to those who took their fingerprints.

One of the comrades, who appeared to be a leader, after listening to the way I spoke to them, asked me to count to a number along the line. He had special instruction about the person who was in line at that number, and dressed in the way the comrade described. He went on to advise me that when it came to the person's turn, I should not show that I suspected that there was something amiss with the arrests. As far as the comrade was concerned, that person was a police informant. They even suspected that he was the one who informed the police as to where they would be found and attacked.

When the person's turn came, he told me that his game was to make fools of Inkatha warlords and the police. His game was getting information from Inkatha as to where they would hold their meetings and where they had planned attacks on the UDF.

That man was Katiza Cebekhulu, who, just about the same time, showed up in Soweto as a member of the Mandela Football Club, and later became the subject of a book[2].

What happened in Mpumalanga Township was a massacre where eleven comrades were killed, allegedly by Inkatha's Caprivi-trained killers, backed by members of the South African security forces.

---

2 The book, *Katiza's Journey*, was written by Fred Bridgland and published by Sidgwick & Jackson Ltd in 1997

Chapter 27
The Third Force

There was quite a debate about whether it was or was not there. When black people engaged in confrontations among themselves in South African unrest situations, they triggered the question of its existence or non-existence. These confrontations resulted in large-scale killings of one another for reasons that were not very clear.

When it was tribal factions fighting, it was clear, and it could be explained. The difficultly was when the conflicts were political.

When tribal factions fought it could easily be traced to competition among Zulu tribal dance groups over allocation of land, or suitors coming and winning the love of a young maiden from an area outside the suitor's local area. It could have been about stock theft or allegations of the existence of wizards or witches in a particular community or among a particular clan. It could also have been over inheritance, pitting siblings against one another. When these were not controlled and allowed to become revenge killings then they became full-blown faction fights. These resulted in deaths at alarming scales, known as black on black tribal conflicts.

Once there was politics involved in a South African conflict situation, and particularly in the one I had occasion to witness first hand, there was doubts on where I stood. It was not clear whether fighting among blacks, where many innocent people were killed and where the duration of the killings was unlimited and seemingly timed to coincide with certain political events, could be called black on black violence. There were facts indicating clearly that it was not the case.

I was in KwaZulu Natal from the beginning of the conflict between the Inkatha organization and the United Democratic Front (UDF), until the end. I was not only a policeman, a member of the South African Police Force, but also a detective, who was directly involved in some of the major cases with the two political organizations. My involvement had to do with criminal offences that members of these parties had committed. There were members of the Security Branch and other security forces engaged in the political aspect of the unrest. My job description included investigating murders, kidnappings, rapes, robberies, and the burning and destruction of property.

Some members' political actions caused them to be caught up in our line of duty and they suffered the consequences. Likewise, some of our police colleagues who acted similarly suffered the same consequences. Somewhere in the chapters of this book, details of that are narrated. The Truth and Reconciliation Commission's (TRC) files contain the bulk of that testimony. Those files also answer very clearly the question of whether there was or was not a third force. This question was demystified beyond any ambiguity. The sad part of the whole notion of black on black violence is that it was so satanically crafted, so much so, that some of the gullible victims were so hooked that they were prepared to lose their lives, without ever stopping to ponder the wisdom of their sacrifices.

The two thousand and more black people who died in the so-called black on black violence in KwaZulu Natal, died in vain. Nothing was achieved through those deaths.

To further illustrate how the so-called black on black violence was orchestrated, one need not look further than at the delivery of tons of deadly weapons to KwaZulu Natal at the height of the so called black on black conflict. Those were remnants of weapons from Namibia, which had been used in the killing of blacks there during the struggle by SWAPO against apartheid security forces. The weapons were delivered to KwaZulu Natal for the sole purpose of killing blacks.

It was the responsibility of the South African Police to investigate the list of over four hundred Inkatha members in leadership positions who were killed during the conflict, without the perpetrators ever having been brought to justice. All the intelligence institutions involved, including those of the KwaZulu Government, with the capacity they had, for some reason 'failed' to use their combined power to solve even one of those cases. They were the ones who failed Inkatha, for reasons known only to themselves.

Lining up security forces in terms of who they were in favour of, gives a very clear picture as to the deliberate failure of those forces to deliver on the list of the four hundred Inkatha victims. The KwaZulu Police had their uniform branch with powers equal to any in South Africa. They had their own Detective Branch, with investigative and arrest powers anywhere in KwaZulu Natal. They had what was called the BSI, which was their intelligence-gathering component. They had the special constables who also did some ground work activity. In addition, there were the so-called Caprive-Trained Units, some of whom were known to participate in the KwaZulu Natal violence, and were convicted for such in some cases. There were the South African Police Uniformed members, the Detective Branch, with the murder and robbery units, the Security Branch gathering political intelligence, as well as the unrest units, dealing directly with political violence.

This lethal combination of pro-Inkatha forces, with the awesome capacity at their disposal, could only fail if they wanted to; or they had never intended to make any effort to solve the cases. Together, they did not have a reputation for failing to deal with those kinds of situations.

Having said all this, how does one dismiss the ever lingering suspicion that this was part of the manifestation of the third force, trying by all means, to market to the gullible, its lame excuse that it was all black on black violence, when in fact, it was a baby of their own orchestration.

The South African National Congress (ANC) and United Democratic Front (UDF) fought apartheid from all angles and with all they had, including their lives. They were banned, arrested, detained, tortured, incarcerated and, in many instances, killed. They met death in many animalistic and barbaric ways, hanged, poisoned, suffocated, thrown through the windows of high buildings, fed to crocodiles, lured to spots where they were shot and buried in shallow graves on farms all over the country. None of these things happened to their adversaries, because those adversaries never fought apartheid. Those who fought injustice, to gain liberation for the suffering masses of black people, confronted the apartheid regime head on.

On the other hand, apartheid forces created a situation where certain blacks in the provinces of South Africa were selected and given so-called 'states' within South Africa, all part of the land over which the ANC, UDF, PAC and AZAPO were fighting. The liberation forces found themselves having to fight to break down the devious mini states and to reunite a free South Africa for all South Africans who lived in it.

Those who had been handed mini states and mini armies, all of which were financed by the apartheid government, armed themselves to protect their mini states. For the abhorrent regime, this was necessary because when the freedom fighters engaged the whole apartheid setup, including the mini states, the apartheid state used the mini states strategically. When some thought they were supposedly protecting their states, they were actually protecting apartheid South Africa. Because they were black, they killed and were killed by blacks. They became allies of the apartheid security forces. Black mini states protected what they had gotten by default. They had no option but to depend on apartheid security forces fighting the liberation forces on their side. Blacks killed blacks because of apartheid!

The fact of the matter is that none of the mini states officials and other beneficiaries ever tasted incarceration, banning or death at the hands of the apartheid security forces because of the fact they did not fight apartheid in whose hands the freedom of the black masses of South Africa rested.

The beauty of it all is that when the ANC won, it did what it had always been fighting for: to free all South Africans from the yoke of oppression under colonialism and apartheid. It brought the mini states back into the fold of a truly united democratic South Africa. The ANC understood that they were victims of a cruel plan by the National Party government to rule blacks by dividing them, so that they use others as cannon fodder in bloody battles against one another. These battles were intended to decrease the number of black people in South Africa or possibly eliminate them or reduce them to little pockets of species on the verge of extinction.

The ANC forgave everybody. They forgave the apartheid government and those black people they used against other black people in their dirty war to protect and preserve apartheid. Everybody was forgiven because everybody was used.

Hitler used Germans to destroy Germany. The world forgave the Nazis, except for those who were tried in the Nuremberg Trials that followed. South Africa's' little Hitlers tried to destroy South Africa, using South Africans. South Africans forgave apartheid except for the slapping on the knuckles with the Black Economic Empowerment (BEE).

Chapter 28
Five Bodies Under the Paradise Bridge

There was a time when it became a habit with senior detective officers in charge in our Durban West District office to call upon me to assist in the investigation of complicated and serious cases in the area. Sometimes I would be called alone and asked to form my own group of detectives to work with me on particular investigations. Sometimes I would be teamed up with white detectives.

One of those cases happened when game rangers were walking in thick bush at a place called Paradise Valley between Pinetown and Durban. They were shocked to see five dead bodies of young black men. They reported to the police and an investigation commenced. The five bodies were found under the Paradise Valley Bridge in a local nature reserve. The case was allocated to a young black sergeant at Pinetown to investigate. After having studied the case, he felt that it would be beyond his experience and asked to be relieved of it. His request was granted.

The case was then handed over to me to investigate. It was obvious that it needed much more skill and expertise. It had also been obvious that the bodies had been thrown over the bridge on the western high way from Durban to Johannesburg. It was clear that it was not a one-man operation and it was an act that needed logistics, manpower and planning by people with a very serious motive. It was not clear whether the people were thrown over the bridge alive, or were killed somewhere else and only brought there to be disposed of.

What was clear was that, whatever motivated their killers, it was so engrossing that they could undertake such a dare-devil operation. It could have been accompanied by blinding or calculated hatred by the killers. Killing the five seemed to have been not cruel enough, and disposing of them in the manner they did was to be a cherry on top.

When I applied my own analysis to the case, I felt that assigning a single junior black detective to investigate, despite all the signs that it was very serious and complicated, was plainly suspect. Even giving the case to me, without any suggestion of a team, made me feel that the casual approach by our authorities was not a simple coincidence.

I took a silent vow to turn the tables, go out there, and no matter what, solve the case. It was always within my character to take on cases with challenges. I said to myself, that this was one such a case that presented me with a challenge.

I went to the headquarters to ask for permission to get detective Sgt. Zuma of the firearms unit to join me. I knew him from my days at Mayville Police Station, where he was one of the senior black detectives who taught me detective work. Sgt. Zuma was a member of the murder and robbery unit long before he went to the firearms unit.

It was agreed that I would work with him on the case officially. We had always yearned to work together over the years. We were so happy that, at last, that time had come.

We studied the five murder dockets from Paradise Valley. We came upon information that one of the bodies found under the Paradise Valley Bridge was from Inanda and established that his mother was a domestic worker in Ridge Road.

We went looking for and found her in Ridge Road. She told us that her son was always involved with the police at C. R. Swart Police Station and he was always getting arrested and then released. She went on to say that the last time he was arrested they had told him that that was the last that he would go home alive again. He had come home, having been severely beaten up by the police who had arrested him. He was vomiting blood and was sick to a degree that he had to be treated by his mother's employer who was a medical doctor.

She had not seen her after the last arrest until news of his body being found under the bridge reached her. According to the mother, he was involved with a gang that robbed white people at the beach front in Durban. It was alleged that they killed some of their victims. It appeared like a vicious cycle given that they could be arrested, sent for trial and, after winning their cases, they would go back to their 'game' of robbing tourists at the beach front.

We left her to confirm the stories of arrests at C. R. Swart Square Police Station. Indeed we found that the deceased had been arrested and were questioned and released about three days before their bodies were found. We collected copies of the release warrants and went and confirmed the stories with other parents.

We later went to the headquarters to report what we had found. Our preliminary report triggered so much panic and frantic phoning at the Headquarters. We were eventually told to hand over our dockets for those cases and go back to our usual duties at our stations until further notice. That investigation had to stop there and then.

My colleague and I discussed the matter at length. We had created a cordial working relationship with relatives of the victims and promised them that we would solve the cases. So we decided to go to them and tell them that we would not be seeing them on the days we had promised, and that we were off the case till further notice.

There was a big outcry when the relatives heard about that. The mother who worked for the doctor said that her employer had already been talking about pursuing the matter; now that the police who had promised to kill his servant's son had gone on to kill the boy. Then he was told that the detectives likely to solve the case had been stopped.

We discussed with other witnesses who had information about the implication of police in the murders. There was one suspect who had died earlier on, when allegedly being tortured in the offices and we had visited the mortuary to see his body.

The following day we reported to Headquarters that the parents of the deceased were threatening with the help of their employers to take the matter up. We were told to go and we would be informed later as to the decision from Pretoria.

A day later, we were summoned to Headquarters where we were joined by a white captain from Pinetown and a brigadier from Pretoria. The brigadier told us that we were going to work with him and that were to leave no stone unturned in terms of collecting whatever evidence was coming forth in the matter.

We went back to the relatives and parents of the deceased and also some witnesses with whom we had previously spoke because, surprisingly, the statements we had obtained from all the witnesses had disappeared. Clearly, it was an attempt to cover-up the crime and we decided that we would not allow it to happen.

We were mindful of the risk we were taking and the likely consequences thereof, as far as our own lives and careers were concerned because of our uncompromising attitude at the time. There was the likely notion that, as black policemen, we were not expected to follow up on the case. This is because it could be insinuated that we were forgetting our place in doing so. As such, I felt I was set up by the system when the case was given to me.

They perhaps felt that it was time our wings were clipped before further damage to their course. The engineering of our demise, in one way or the other, in a country where people disappeared without trace, died in crossfire mistakes, or from chairs in interrogation rooms, seemed imminent.

When a high-ranking officer tried to stall or shelve the investigation, our point to him was that we would go back to the witnesses and tell them the case had been taken from us. If the witnesses felt we had abandoned them, they would recognize that it was not our decision to do so. We had our own reputation to protect because we were also well known to people in the black communities and in our minds murder was murder and there were no sacred cows. We decided to bite the bullet and see what came next. Indeed we brought the case back to the table.

In the end, a white sergeant and lieutenant were convicted.

That case to us blacks was one of the eye openers in terms of understanding the political landscape in the apartheid set up. The suspects, who were thrown over Paradise Valley, were suspected criminals having allegedly murdered a tourist. They deserved no sympathy from us because of their being black. In my eyes crime was crime, and murder was murder. Those criminals deserved to be arrested, prosecuted and convicted for the crimes they committed at the beach front. They deserved to be removed from society through the proper process. As well, policemen who arrested and killed the suspects deserved to be arrested prosecuted, convicted and likewise removed from society.

We later learnt that the policemen responsible for the murder of the suspects in question had no knowledge of investigating cases of murder. Instead they would assaulted their suspects so severely that when they took them to court for trial it was proved that the so called confessions they had allegedly obtained were as a result of severe assaults on the suspects by the arresting policemen. Consequently, the judges would throw out the cases to the anger and frustration of the police involved. These policemen then foolishly decided not to ever take those suspects to court but get rid of them by killing them.

Chapter 29
Interference by Senior Officers

It came a time when it became very difficult to carry out police work where politics was involved. It was worse in KwaZulu Natal than anywhere else in the country. During the early 1980s, there was intense fighting between Inkatha and the United Democratic Front (UDF). The apartheid regime regarded UDF as the internal wing of the African National Congress (ANC). The problem arose when rogue element of the South African Police aligned themselves with Inkatha.

These internal elements, in fact, took a position to assist Inkatha in the fight. They would arm Inkatha cadres and, in many instances, be part of attacks on UDF individuals, groups, houses and businesses.

The police also trained Inkatha in the use of arms and methods of attack. Ordinary policemen who focused on were carrying out ordinary police duties and never took sides in the dispute between the parties, were viewed by the rogue elements and Inkatha as sympathizing with the UDF/ANC. This is contrary to the fact that those policemen, black and white, who were not part of the rogue element, carried out their work irrespective of the situation. They arrested members or supporters of the UDF upon whom there was evidence of involvement in killing or harming supporters of Inkatha in any way. They took them to court where their fate was determined. The same applied to members and supporters of Inkatha.

Meanwhile, the rogue elements in the police force were one with Inkatha. They went on to interfere with investigations involving Inkatha members and supporters.

There were several such cases in which I was personally involved. The most problematic factor with those cases stemmed from the elements of the police behind the violence. They were senior members, right up to the ranks of senior colonels and brigadiers (Senior Superintendents and Directors, in today's terms). They had such power that it would have been almost impossible to ignore their instructions, even if the instructions were unlawful. For instance, at times they would want important evidence to be suppressed when it was directed at Inkatha supporters or the rogue police under them.

One time, our team, under Captain Frank Dutton, arrested Msizi Hlophe at about five o'clock in the morning. When we got to the office with him, I started to question him about his alleged involvement in the murder of UDF member Zazi Khuzwayo, Mrs. Pearl Shabalala, Nicholus Mkhize, Emmanuel Khuzwayo and the attempted murder of Mr. Obed Mthembu and his wife Zuziwe. It was alleged that he did this under the instructions of Mr. Jamile, an Inkatha leader and a minister in the then KwaZulu Government.

As I proceeded with the interrogation, two brigadiers arrived and occupied the office next to the one I was using. They called me in and asked me what Msizi was saying about Jamile. I told them that I had just started talking to him. They said that they would want to know what he was saying with respect to Mr. Jamile.

The fact was that, there was a team of detectives investigating cases of murder against certain people. Whenever we arrested those who could have been accomplices in any of the murder cases we were investigating, very senior police officers made a point of being very close to the investigation. Then, they demanded feedback on the responses our suspects gave to questions.

In this particular instance, they were very worried, and they kept calling me, almost every five minutes, to ask me what the suspect had said. When they called me for the third time, I told them that what the suspect was telling me amounted to a confession. I added that I had warned him in accordance with the judges' rules, and he had chosen to make a confession before a magistrate. When I said that, they jumped up and wanted to know if he was implicating Mr. Jamile. I told them that he was, and they quickly walked into my interrogation room to look at the suspect.

One of the officers said that the suspect should not be taken to a magistrate to make a statement on that day. He said that I wait until they gave such an instruction, perhaps the following day.

I told the officers that it will be difficult for me to do that because, when the matter went to court, I would be asked to state what the suspect had said to me during the interrogation. I continued that if I were to say that when the suspect had expressed a willingness to make his statement before a magistrate, instead of arranging for him to be taken to a magistrate I waited until the next day, I would be required to explain my reasons for that decision. I suggested that, to save me a lot of trouble with the court, they put that instruction in writing. I told them that the court was aware that no detective would hesitate to take a statement where a suspect offered to make a confession to a magistrate, especially in a serious matter like the one I was dealing with. They insisted that the suspect should not be taken to a magistrate for a confession on that day.

When, in the end, the suspect made a statement to a magistrate, it had completely changed from what he had told me. The high-ranking officers wanted to know from me who else had made a statement implicating Mr. Jamile. I told them that Mr. Ntshalintshali had also made such a statement. Actually, he had been the one who initiated the investigation, by reporting what he had heard, seen and done, as Mr. Jamile's official driver. He had actually reported the matter to the detective officer who was then the branch commander at the KwaDabeka Police Station. That police station served KwaDabeka Township, the hostel and parts of Clermont Township where Mr. Jamile's alleged murder victims were residing at the time.

When I told the interfering high-ranking officers who were against the investigation concerning Mr. Jamile and supporters or members of Inkatha that Mr. Ntshalintshali had made a statement implicating Mr. Jamile, they instructed me to fetch him and bring him to them. It was clear that they wanted to influence him to change his statement.

When I went for him, he wanted to know why the officers wanted to see him. He said that he had made his statement, and had mentioned all that he knew about Mr. Jamile's alleged criminal activities in relation to the deaths of comrades and UDF supporters in Clermont and KwaDabeka Township. I told him that my feeling was that they wanted to impress upon him to change his statement in as far as it implicated Mr. Jamile and the police.

There had also been information about two white members of the Security Branch from Pinetown who had handed a photo of a comrade from Clermont Township, and alleged that he (the comrade) had been the one who had thrown a bomb into a vehicle in which Mr. Jamile, chief Khawula and Lushaba had been passengers. Chief Lushaba was so seriously injured that he had to undergo a major operation, removing a large part of his lower body.

I indirectly warned Mr. Ntshalintshali against changing his statement, should the officers try to prevail upon him to do so. I also had to be extra careful, because I was aware of offers which could be made to people to change their statements. If they agreed, they would also say that I had advised or warned them.

I took Ntshalintshali from the officers back to where I had picked him up. He went to the City Press Newspaper and told them what I had said to him on our way to the officers. When a photocopy of that report was brought to me with the controversial parts underlined, I anticipated an aggressive reaction from the officers or police headquarters where the copy seemed to have originated.

The fact that nothing was said, and nothing happened by way of summoning me to police headquarters to explain, left me thinking. I could not suppress the suspicion that, the non-reaction meant that a more serious action, more than a disciplinary one, was being seriously contemplated. Nothing was so important about me that if I were seen to be a danger and stumbling block to the aims of the rogue element within the police, there wouldn't be any difficulty in getting rid of me, using any one of the methods on their menu at the time. A sympathizer within the right-wing members of the police force had once told me that my actions were being monitored and that I had to be careful.

Interference Continues

When our team, under Captain Dutton got involved in the Trust Feed Massacre investigation, we arrested Inkatha members who were members of the special constables attached to KwaZulu Police. They were operating with members of the South African Police in the township of Mpumalanga in Hammarsdale and Pietermaritzburg. Their operations involved attacking and killing UDF supporters. They did this mainly through attacking, burning and looting houses.

Comrades were the youth of the UDF, and they were also involved in fights with Inkatha in the townships.

During the Trust Feed Massacre investigation, we were based in a farmhouse between Pietermaritzburg and Wartburg in the Natal Midlands. We picked up information implicating special constables from Mpumalanga, in Hammarsdale, in the Trust Feed massacre. I was later shown a house by a policeman from Hammarsdale police station. He knew that KwaZulu Police special constables, who worked in a unit involved in killing people, used the house.

I went to our base near Wartburg and reported the matter to Captain Dutton and our team. We arranged a raid and found two suspects who led us to Chief Calalakubo Khawula's residence in the South Coast. There we arrested the other suspect who alleged that a senior KwaZulu Police member had sent him there to hide from Ulundi. His name was Ndwalane, and he was a serving member of the KwaZulu Police then, but he was being used in the killing of UDF members.

Later we arrested four black people, who were serving in the KwaZulu Government, Captain Mitchell of the South African Police, and Captain van der Heever of the Riot Unit in Pietermaritzburg, who mostly operated in the conflict or unrest in Mpumalanga Township.

One evening, when I was busy taking a statement from suspect Ndwalane, three senior police officers arrived at our base, a General, a Colonel, and a Captain, all from Pretoria. They demanded to know what the suspect had been saying. I told them that he had given us a statement, which implicated Captain Mitchell, himself and several others involved. I also told them that I was arranging for the suspect to be taken to a magistrate the following day to make a statement.

The general queried the fact that I was taking a statement from the suspect. As far as he was concerned, black policemen were never used for taking statements from suspects, and that blacks were only used as interpreters for white policemen taking statements. They then demanded that the suspect be brought before them for one of them to take the statement, while I interpreted. I told him that I had gone through questioning the suspect and that I had completed his statement. I could not have him make two statements because I was going to be the one giving evidence about what happened when I interrogated him to the court.

I asked them to direct me on what to say about the fact that I was forced to abandon my interrogation because I was only considered to be an interpreter when the court knew me as a detective in charge of an interrogation and not as an interpreter?

They ignored my questions and forced the suspect to answer their questions while I interpreted. The following day, Captain Dutton reported the matter to the Attorney General, Mr. Mike Imber. The senior officers from Pretoria were ordered to leave our investigation alone and they left.

What they were doing by that kind of interference was to protect the policemen and the Inkatha members involved in the massacre of people. The victims had gathered in a house for a wake and were massacred for the simple reason that they were perceived to be UDF members. We learned that the massacre had been planned at Inkatha headquarters in Edendale at a meeting attended by senior police officers of the riot unit, including the station commander of Newhanover Police Station, the Inkatha leader of Trust Feed, and an alleged warlord and police informer.

There was also an Inkatha leader of Pietermaritzburg involved in the planning to attack Trust Feed. A police major and his junior in the riot unit delivered the attacking special constables' team to New Hanover. The whole operation was carried out by South African Police, special constables of KwaZulu Police, and Inkatha warlords of Trust Feed.

None of these people were reprimanded by their organizations or employers for committing crimes of such magnitude, in terms of callousness and crudeness. Imagine there was even a dead body in the room, which was the reason for the wake, when some of those who got shot fell on top of the dead body.

Instead of seeking justice for the victims, senior policemen tried their best, even in court, to protect their own. Those were policemen who were nowhere near serving the cause of justice. They were more deadly than many known criminal. As senior policemen, those who engaged as partners with the Inkatha in the war with the UDF/ANC, they were untouchables in terms of the difficulty there was in doubting, or resisting their instructions, even though the instructions were unlawful.

Our team in Pietermaritzburg demonstrated our intention not to comply with the illegal suggestion by the three brigadiers. We had secretly taken a stand that we were not going to kill anyone from either the UDF or Inkatha. We went ahead and arrested those of Inkatha who had been influenced to think that murder was no longer a crime when the victims were UDF supporters. They were apparently serving that cause when they went and killed Mr. Nkomo, an old man, and a member of a trade union, despite the fact that he had won an interdict protecting him from being threatened, attacked or killed. Our team arrested the offenders, took them to court and they were convicted. The judge presiding over the case commended us for a job well done.

One evening, I was present at a warlord's house in Pietermaritzburg when about three supposed Inkatha hit-squad members reported to the warlord. They were in the presence of one of the brigadiers. We were told about the plan to get rid of the leadership of the UDF/ANC who were behind the comrades responsible for driving Inkatha from their areas surrounding Pietermaritzburg. Their report was that they had been to Mr. Chettys' house, but he was not there. They had been wearing trade union T-shirts and were welcomed by Mrs. Chetty, who offered them tea. Mr. Chetty was one of the leaders on the list that Sichizo Zuma read out to us. He had come with the brigadiers to the meeting to discuss getting rid of UDF/ANC leaders. After our unit had left Pietermaritzburg, the fighting seemed to have changed, in that the rate of deaths had been reduced to one or two deaths per week and some weeks none at all. That was also the reason it was decided that we moved on.

Chapter 30
Kwa Ndebele the Stinking Skunk in its True Colours

I thought I had seen it all, but the worst was yet to come. I had just witnessed one of the dirtiest and most cruel acts of the apartheid security agents.

One evening in 1986, they entered a house in Chesterville, a small township in the western south of the city of Durban. They claimed to have come from the ANC's armed wing to help comrades there with arms to fend off their Inkatha enemies. They tricked the occupants to leave the main house so that they could be shown how to use the weapons. All the occupants moved to an outside building on the property.

While all the boys were inside the hut, the security agents fired from outside, killing all four of them.

Although it was late at night, I was sent there from the Durban Westville Prison, where I had been busy with investigative duties. There were heartrending wails of anguish and extreme pain from relatives, neighbours and friends of the deceased.

It was a horrific sight, heavy with the smell of fresh human blood. The very sight of that nerve-shuttering scene drained me of my years of courage and experience. Disgracefully, even as a hardened detective, I found myself struggling to hold back tears.

Those were young innocent members of a community, looking forward to doing their part in protecting themselves, their families and their community, and they were targeted by outside forces. Their only sin was that they were not willing to embrace their own enslavement; that they supported the anti-apartheid movement, the UDF.

When I spoke to one of the people gathered around the scene, I was informed that, before the shooting started, a number of vehicles were seen parked at a circle just above the property, but they were out of sight. Many police vehicles and police video trucks, including an ambulance, were seen parked as if in the ready, and clearly anticipating something major happening. They were seen by the people as a back-up to what had been certain to happen.

I tried to approach some people for statements but they were not prepared to talk to me. They said that they thought I was part of the force. They had been recently attacked by policemen so how would they know that I was not part of the group parked at the circle above. Indeed, how could they tell I was not just like those policemen who were running up and down at the scene taking photos. I may have been there to add insult to their minds – the insult that was carried out by the police who were pretending to investigate the heinous crimes this constituted.

Ironically, I had been alerted of the shooting by a member of the Security Branch who was on duty in their offices next to ours at the Durban Westville prison. That evening, they had been working night duty, just as we were. He, of course, knew the plan around that incident.

When I returned from the scene, it was the Security Branch person who told me that he had been told that the victims' family had suspected involvement by the police. According to him, it could not be true, because he had just received information that the mini bus used by the killers was stolen from the Free State, which meant that those people were just criminals.

Later, I received notification that I was required to report at Police National Headquarters in Pretoria in order to meet the National Detective Commissioner, who had a job of investigation for me in Kwa Ndebele. I was puzzled, and felt very uneasy. I had not done or achieved any miraculous feat as a detective that would cause anyone to leave all their well-known, tried-and-tested specialists and go for a simple warrant officer from, of all places, KwaZulu Natal. They wanted me to deal with Sotho, Ndebele and Afrikaans-speaking people, in a province known for its extremes. I really smelled the proverbial rat in the whole set up.

From my point of view, I was concerned, because there was an absence of any plausible motive for choosing me for that monumental case. Beyond the proverbial yellow lights that I saw in front of me, I could also see red lights flickering in the not-so-distant future. I could envision those red lights, at one point or another, being less than inches away. That was what bothered me as I set out on my adventurous and dangerous journey to a 'mission impossible'.

I was given a brand-new Ford motor car for the journey, which still needed to be turned in. I kept my speed at 100 km and less all the way to Pretoria. I was accommodated for the night at the white police training college. In the morning, I drove to the National Police

Headquarters to meet the Detectives General, who was in charge of all detectives in the country. It had been stated in the documents of my invitation that I would report to him.

When I got to his office, I was told that the General had already left for Kwa Ndebele, that he had flown in a helicopter and that he had left instructions that I be escorted there. There were two white detectives waiting to drive me to where he was. I found that most things had been arranged, including people who would give me all the support I would need while I was in Kwa Ndebele. Two members of the Security Branch were to drive me to Kwa Ndebele in the car in I had used from Durban.

I found the detectives in their office with a black colleague who had shining, brushed-back hair. They were talking about people who were threatening to take them to court for assault. The black one said, "They can do that if they want their witnesses to disappear forever."

I began to think that those could be dangerous people. It was very unsettling to think that I was going to travel 120 km with them from Pretoria to Kwa Ndebele. I wondered if they would indeed take me to Kwa Ndebele to meet the General, or somewhere else to meet my Maker.

The two young men spoke Afrikaans, and they oozed arrogant patriotism. When I told them that I would prefer if they used their car to take me to Kwa Ndebele, because mine had been on the road for about three days and still needed running, they did not respond. They pretended that they had not heard me, got into my car, asked for the keys and away we drove off.

As soon as we got onto the free-way to Kwa Ndebele, the driver put his foot down and pushed the speed to 120km/h. It became senseless to protest. As we drove, he saw a restaurant on the roadside and he stopped the car and went inside. Another car driven by what appeared to be a friend of theirs parked next to our car, and they exchanged greetings. The friend expressed surprise that the other one was still driving after the very serious accident he had recently been involved in. It appeared to me that the way he was driving even then, could easily lead to a fatal accident.

He returned with three hot pies and three cokes and divided them among us. As soon as he hit the road again, the speedometer pin swept across the face to rest on the last figure on the right, and it remained there. Through the rear-view mirror, he saw me fighting for my seat belt as I swayed from left to right, and I saw him exchange smiles with his friend. Until then, smiles had been a scarce commodity throughout our fate-tempting journey. I had forgotten that the car was supposed to have been taken for service; I was now too preoccupied with my own survival and the engine would see to its own.

My mind flashed back to when our reckless driver emerged from the restaurant with three pies and three cokes for the three of us to share, and I thought, 'Perhaps this guy is no more dangerous than just being a speed freak; I could give him a point on the stakes of humanity, just this once.' I felt that, it was not necessary to speculate further about him.

I prayed silently for our safe arrival at wherever we were headed; it was a prayer for all three of us. My conscience dictated that his gesture of the three cokes and three pies qualified him for inclusion in my prayer. After all, I thought he might just have been a victim of a fantasy that he was a race car driver. Such an obsession might sometimes drive him nuts, if it was true that he had just survived a major accident, according to his friend who had found us at the restaurant on the freeway. That had been said in his absence any way. As far as he was concerned, to me, he had a clean record as far as dangerous driving was concerned.

He seemed to derive fun from seeing me scared. The best I could do under the circumstances was to keep my complaining and whining silently to myself. The reality was that, at that moment and until we reached our destination, my fate was in his hands.

We managed to reach Kwa Ndebele miraculously, safely. As soon as we entered Kwa Ndebele, there was no mistaking that we had entered a war zone. There were police and soldiers everywhere conducting roadblock inspections and some were just patrolling shopping centres.

We could see houses that were burnt down to ashes. Young men, or comrades as they were popularly known, were obviously in hiding somewhere because they were not on the roads.

We drove straight to the Kwa Ndebele Police Headquarters. We entered a hall where there was an officers' meeting chaired by the General. The General was addressing the police officers deployed in Kwa Ndebele to deal with the grave unrest.

Immediately our driver got into the hall, I saw all the other police officers leave the hall to mill around the yard, the passages and the veranda. Some were smoking and others wondering what was so important that the General would stop his meeting with them in order to talk to me in private. They were very high-ranking officers and all white. I had never in my life seen a situation like that.

I just wondered what the world was turning out to be for me. A one-on-one, face-to-face meeting, with the General in charge of the country's detectives and me, a warrant officer, a black one at that, and from of all places, KwaZulu Natal!

One of the General's aides ushered me inside. I saluted the General and he directed me to sit down. I was dressed in my best suit; the one I knew also made me look dignified and presentable. He was calm and collected, and had, as it were, 'authority' written all over him. He spoke slowly and very clearly, as he disclosed what he wanted and expected me to do in Kwa Ndebele. He said the South African Government had given authority to Kwa Ndebele, to form a government, have a parliament, and run the country in preparation for full independence, if they so wished.

He said it all went smoothly until some cabinet ministers got involved in corruption and serious crime. The South African government had come to a conclusion that they should be investigated thoroughly. If evidence so dictated, they should be arrested, charged and taken to court. He said the main culprit was the Minister of the Interior, Mr. Piet Ntuli. He said that Kwa Ndebele was getting out of control with a lot of people dying daily.

There was a kind of full-scale war between the U.D.F comrades and Imbokodo Party warlords, of which, some of the ministers were part. He said he would be coming to Kwa Ndebele every fortnight for progress reports from me. He stressed the fact that I was to answer to him and only him while conducting that investigation. I would be provided with support when I needed it. I would also be provided with accommodation in one of the riot Police bases.

When we finished the meeting I was driven to the base where it turned out there were detectives, high-ranking detective officers, who were doing unrest-related investigations in Kwa Ndebele. For our office work, we were to share one large building which appeared to have been an old farmhouse. The office appeared to have been a lounge or living room for the high-ranking detective officers. However, the black sergeant who was my driver, and I, would share the outbuilding, formerly the servants' quarters.

There were six murder dockets for my immediate attention. There were six comrades who were killed when their areas were surrounded by the police and soldiers and then attacked by Imbokodo warlords. The warlords included cabinet ministers, prominent among were:

Piet Ntuli and George Majozi Mahlangu. One of the areas invaded was under Chief Msebenzi Mahlangu. The areas invaded were the G and H sections in Tweefontein.

The invasion happened on June 12, 1986. It was said that Piet Ntuli amassed a great deal of wealth in Kwa Ndebele's large shopping centres. The problem was that, in the fight between the comrades and Imbokodo (Ntuli party), the comrades had burnt down all the shopping centres and Piet Ntuli declared war on them. It was a war of extremes, very ugly and very unbalanced. It was clouded with a multiplication of confusion. There were kidnappings, neck lacings, shootings, rapes, burning and general mayhem. It was all a crazy experiment gone terribly wrong. Nobody knew who exactly the enemy was and why a country, on the brink of supposed freedom, was suddenly on the brink of its own destruction.

Kwa Ndebele was a homeland of the poorest of the poor. It was a real church mouse 'country', if you like. The conflict in the homeland was similar to what pertained in Kwa Zulu Natal, in the sense that from the UDF side there were comrades, just like the situation in Kwa Ndebele. Adults and businessmen from the Inkatha had become warlords, something many did as a way of protecting their businesses, and others did so to fight for their organization.

The South African Police and some elements of the army manipulated the unrest in both Inkatha and Imbokodo. There had always been an outcry, from the UDF and other organizations pursuing for peace, that there was a third party involved in the conflict. Equally, there had been denials regarding these 'insinuations'. As an investigator in the in Kwa Zulu Natal's supposed black on black conflict and violence, I was in a position to see things clearly in Kwa Ndebele.

What I saw in Kwa Ndebele was, in many respects, a carbon copy of what was happening in Kwa Zulu Natal. The difference was that in Kwa Zulu Natal there were no cabinet ministers running and chasing comrades, and physically invading comrade areas shooting and burning houses. That was left to individual warlords in the townships around cities, and some outlying rural areas.

In Kwa Zulu Natal, cabinet ministers were more mature, sophisticated and experienced than those of Kwa Ndebele. Occasionally, one could find physical involvement of a cabinet minister in the murder of UDF murders.

However, the wanton loss of lives in both Kwa Ndebele and Kwa Zulu Natal were not as a result of a black on black conflict. It was the apartheid government's clumsily hidden war against the UDF and ANC. I saw it all, and played a part in exposing it.

In short, Inkatha warlords and hit squads on one hand, and members of the UDF and comrades on the other hand as well as many others in their communities, died in a war which was not theirs. It is those that remotely controlled the way who insisted that it was a black on black conflict. Why would it have been that all the black people suffering bitter and dehumanizing oppression at the hands of the white racists' apartheid supporters, decided to ignore, and at the worst even embrace, the very source of their suffering, and turn against their own fellow blacks and fellow sufferers? Why?

I figured out for myself that the power of the unseen chose a deliberate strategic position for me to be where I would clearly hear and see whatever there was to hear and see. The National Party had been in government for ten years. They were just beginning to implement the evil politics of apartheid when I arrived on the scene of the South African Police Force.

The Kwa Ndebele situation was very sinister and complicated, as far as the unrest was concerned. I felt I had to move carefully. I was trapped in a web of intrigue. My clients, as it were, were the comrades, most of whom were in wheelchairs as a result of being shot by Imbokodo, the police or the soldiers. Some had been kidnapped earlier and taken to a distant bush, where they were forced to make a huge fire and walk with their bare feet on the glowing coals. They got burnt so severely that some became disabled, acts the army and police allegedly perpetrated.

My witnesses were comrades on the cases where some were murdered and others seriously injured. The police were arresting them for what they were alleged to have done to shops belonging to members of the Imbokodo, and also for murders and rapes. Imbokodo police and the army were harassing them. This made my mission of collecting evidence against the Imbokodo warlords, some of whom were cabinet ministers, very difficult.

In doing my work, I became the enemy of Imbokodo and some policemen, as if I represented the comrades. But I needed their evidence to do my work. I was investigating cabinet ministers who were members of the Imbokodo and were helping the Imbokodo. Indeed, the whole thing was a real concoction of mayhem.

I was given a black police warrant officer, Fani Molapo, to look after me in Kwa Ndebele. He seemed to have been given strict instructions with regard to assisting and taking care of me. He carried them out with excellence during my entire stay in Kwa Ndebele. He had a football club which was composed of some police players and local boys. He made it a point, in his effort to see to my comfort and pleasure, to take me along to watch his football club, wherever they played on weekends.

Sometimes Fani Molapo would take me all the way to Johannesburg to watch matches between big clubs such as Kaizer Chiefs and Orlando Pirates. He would invite me to dinner at his house, where my clothes would also be ironed. In addition, he introduced me to the then leader of the comrades in Kwa Ndebele, the late Mr. James Mahlangu of the Royal Palace, who later became a member of parliament in the new democratic government.

Fani Molapo traced all the comrades and businessmen who had evidence against Imbokodo's corrupt members and accused of murder. He collected all the comrades from whom I took statements, and sometimes the debriefing was done in his house. He would trace comrades wherever they were hiding. He would then make arrangements for meetings with me. He turned my mission impossible to be possible and accomplishable.

Kwa Ndebele was a mixed bag of untoward happenings. One day, at one of the schools, pupils and teachers saw white soldiers putting up tents and tables in the school sports ground and even a Red Cross sign, as if a mobile clinic was going to be operated. As soon as the tents were in placed and all seemed ready, suddenly Imbokodo men and some soldiers armed with sjamboks, surrounded the school. They attacked and whipped the children and teachers with the sjamboks, and in the process inflicting severe injuries on most of them. To complete the most amazing show ever seen by anyone there, the marauders collected all the injured pupils and teachers, placed them into the tents and army nurses and doctors got busy attending to their injuries.

The medical team gave injections to the more serious ones, and stitched and bandaged the others.

It is worth noting that as the perpetrators sjamboked the pupils and their teachers, some of the assailants, the Imbokodo, were saying that they were giving that school a good lesson, because the schools and the teachers there were all comrades. The assailants said the same was going to be the case with all schools that harboured comrades. They said that Imbokodo was on a mission to rid Kwa Ndebele of all comrades.

I started investigations in the case and took statements from teachers, some of whom were admitted in hospital because of the severity of the injuries they had sustained as a result of the attack.

The acts were perpetrated by Imbokodo and the soldiers, some of who were in Kwa Ndebele to help and protect the innocent. However, instead, accompanied by some notorious Imbokodo killers, who featured prominently in many acts of the unrest in Kwa Ndebele, they attacked and wounded the same innocent people they were to protect. At that point, Kwa Ndebele was completely lawless. Imbokodo ruled by the sjambok and the gun. Kwa Ndebele's own policemen were completely ineffective. Imbokodo was in charge.

By the way, Imbokodo was the brainchild of someone in Pretoria with a view to destabilizing political activism against apartheid, with the UDF as the main target. Pretoria knew that the target of the UDF's anti-apartheid activism was the seat of apartheid in Pretoria. Imbokodo would be made to die defending apartheid for the bosses in Pretoria.

On its part, the UDF would not lie down and let that happen. Liberation was too big a goal to abandon because of hired goons and hungry adventurers, ready to sell their souls and people in a game of chance they did not, and never would, understand. Pretorias' game was not a child's' play, and not for toddlers crawling to a fire, thinking it was candy. When Imbokodo was presented with a party and a government, they thought it was all going to be rosy. They did not know that they were being presented with a war they could not win.

*****

When I had collected the evidence required to make a case in court, I sent a message to the General to ask for reinforcements for the planned arrest for Mr. Piet Ntuli and some of his cabinet members. I also suggested what I thought would be a suitable date.

When the General came to Kwa Ndebele, I discussed the matter with him. Somehow I think the information was deliberately leaked. One afternoon, two days before the intended arrest, I saw a warrant officer in the office of the brigadier in charge of investigations. He was telling the brigadier that Piet Ntuli was saying that he was aware of his pending arrest. As he spoke, I was behind him. He had not noticed me. He reported all Piet Ntuli had said and that Ntuli was asking that he should not be arrested by the black detective from Kwa Zulu Natal. That would humiliate him, and if it happened, he would spill the beans, and would not go to jail alone. The senior officer told the warrant officer that I reported directly to the General from headquarters in Pretoria.

The following day, in the morning just before all those working outside left the radio and telephone attended, a black constable was handed a brown envelope and told that he should hand it over to some people who would come from Pretoria.

I had a black policeman who drove me around in Kwa Ndebele, and as usual, that morning we drove along the main Kwa Ndebele road in the direction of Pretoria. I saw a car travelling at a very high speed. It flashed its lights at us, and my driver responded by doing the same. He then remarked that those people in the car driving to Kwa Ndebele were from Pretoria and that they did not come to Kwa Ndebele unless somebody was going to be taken out. At that time the expression 'taken out' was often used by policemen, meaning 'killed'. He then found a spot and made a U-turn. We proceeded back to our office and he told me that he wanted to prove something.

At the office, we found only the black constable who had been handed an envelope. My driver asked if the people from Pretoria had not arrived. The answer was no. My driver then picked up the envelope and opened it. It had not been sealed and out came a photo of a black man, who he said was Piet Ntuli. We left the office and proceeded with our work. The reason the car we had met had not been picked up the photo was that, it appeared, they first drove into the Sibuswa administrative offices or police headquarters. All day, my driver kept telling me that somebody was going to be taken out that day. We returned to our base and our sleeping quarters in the evening.

When we were about to sleep there was a noise in the garage and the three senior officers who slept in the main house left. About 4 o'clock the next morning my driver woke me up and asked that we drive to Siyabuswa. When we got close to the bridge of a rivulet which was then a dry *donga*, we saw a lot of police cars with lights flashing and warning people or drivers not to advance to the bridge. Lights were flashing all over the place and the bridge area was cordoned off.

We produced our police cards and ventured close to the bridge. Right there, Piet's car was on the bridge and was perforated all over. The roof was almost missing and the engine was lying down in the *donga* on the bottom of the river. Pieces of human flesh hung from the branches of the trees close by. Shoes and pieces of what he was wearing were also hanging there. My suspect, Piet Ntuli, had been in a car bomb explosion that night. This was one day before I had planned he should be arrested.

About sunrise, information filtered through that Piet Ntuli had just left a late meeting with the police in the hall, when he somehow got delayed until he was the only one left behind. He left alone, heading towards the bridge. He was not to cross it that day, as he had always done many times before. This time he was to exit his car through its perforated and blown- up roof. This time it was to be in pieces of flying flesh that landed on nearby trees, in the worst kind of death. That was clearly the work of heartless beasts, masquerading as human beings.

A General, the head of all detectives in the country, had instructed me to investigate Piet Ntuli for the purpose of going to court. When I was about to arrest the suspect, Security Branch detectives, serving under the same General, decided, before I spoke to him, to silence him by killing him. To add salt to the raw wound, an inquest docket was opened to be investigated by detectives who were present at the meeting where plans of his murder were discussed. As if that were not bizarre enough, a *braai* was organized in Kwa Ndebele, where the murderers and the investigators celebrated together, drinking themselves silly with litres and litres of liquor, all the way from Pretoria.

If you think you have heard it all, you are wrong! I, the investigating officer, was part of the *braai*, having been instructed to go to a farm away from Siyabuswa with my driver, to prepare the fire for the *braai*. This, in a way, demonstrated that in the minds of those people, I did not exist, and if they thought I did, I was only a zombie from some zoo from Kwa Zulu. They were so intoxicated in their fantasy world that they had memory lapses of any reality. At the time, they were deserted by all tenets that together constituted a complete human being with the ability to distinguish right from wrong.

I do not know what made them think that I did not know they had killed my suspect. Now wait for the last bit.

My clients, the comrades, celebrated the death of Piet Ntuli for the whole week. Upon hearing the news of his death, the comrades went to his farms, collected his cattle and divided them among the areas with each herd consisting not less than five beasts. They then slaughtered these cattle as part of their 'celebration' spree.

Meanwhile, the perpetrators of the murder must have thought so lowly of me that they imagined my feeble mind would make anything of it. It was rather audacious on their part to kill my suspect, and then order me to make a fire for them to *braai*, meet and watch them celebrate his murder.

Seeing how apartheid turned white people into addicts of wrong-doing, and how they derived pleasure at the sight of the blood of others, was the apex of my sinfulness, regardless of one's religion.

In my own way, I was one of the of people who tried to send messages to alert the ANC that this was not for them to celebrate as something they had achieved. The comrades were also convinced that some comrades somewhere, or those in exile, had done it.

*****

I went to see my comrades celebrating at Chief Msebenzi Mahlangu's great palace because I had taken statements from victim comrades and witnesses. For them, it was celebration over the Piet Ntuli's death. Some of his cattle were awaiting slaughter in the kraal, and some had been slaughtered and the meat was cooking in large three-legged pots and the rest was on huge fires being *braised*. I was offered a place among the chiefs and respected locals, and participated in the *braai*. Nothing can adequately describe the wild, ecstatic mood of that time. My driver was at the chief's great palace with me, because he had driven me there. He actually belonged to the Security Branch, the people who had murdered my suspect, Piet Ntuli. They were his colleagues. That is why they had flicked lights for us on the day we met them racing to Kwa Ndebele. That is why, as an insider, he knew their presence there meant someone was going to be 'taken out', as he had put it. That is why he had turned back to see whose photo was in the envelope that had been left for killers in our office.

I recalled that on our way to prepare the fire for the officer's *braai*, and as we drove through farms in a two-wheel farm road, he let out what I took seriously and thought hard over. He said, "the place we are going to is strictly for trusted people, and nobody comes back from there should he be slightly suspected of being disloyal, alone be inclined to either UDF or ANC."

I started to suspect that 'this was my day', the one I had thought hard about. I responded, "I am aware of the precariousness of my situation and I have got it all covered. Every day and hour of my presence in Kwa Ndebele is in the hands of people who would be alerted of my disappearance." In that moment, I found myself getting angry but also sweating. I was in fear. I felt that even when I presented a bold appearance, I knew that I was trapped.

As we made the journey, I thought of shooting him while he was driving, and escape with the van. On further thought, I realized that it would be futile because the road was such that I could not turn and drive in a different direction; it was a one-way 'street' and would be used by the convoy of officers going to the *braai*. I imagined I would abandon that van and run off on foot as soon as they discovered his dead body. Dog squads and helicopters would be out and I would not have a chance running between the short thorn bushes, let alone getting tired.

We drove in silence for a while and he looked at me and said not to bother, as he was just joking. I said he should not pin anything to what I had said because I was only returning his joke. There was a thin thread of tension hanging in the air for a while, and when it cleared, things became normal.

The spot where we got to was a hut in the middle of nowhere and I wondered who would go there, and from where and for what? There were thick cardboard boxes spread on the floor, as if someone slept there. He openly said that it was a torture house, and proudly said that whoever was brought there for interrogation would either tell the whole truth or die. We put together large logs of very dry wood and prepared a braai fire.

All the officers came and the *braai* started. I had a beer. Soon after, the driver and I left and returned to our camp near Siyabuswa.

We later learned how drunk the officers got at the *braai* and there was some drama as well, the kind that goes with heavy drinking. And there was more to follow.

Thereafter, and in a very abrupt manner, we were told to leave Kwa Ndebele immediately. I was directed to hand over all my dockets at the Pretoria Police Headquarters. An officer in Pretoria told me that we had to hand the dockets in because Kwa Ndebele was on the verge of attaining complete independence and that the cases would be handed over to new government to continue with if they so wished.

Promptly, I went to the headquarters and, while there, I was called into a side office where I met an officer who showed me a piece of paper. It was a written invitation by the Kwa Zulu Police to join them as a member of their force. The person who showed me the invitation said his only duty was to inform me of its contents, get me to comment and sign, and that he would then return it to Kwa Zulu.

I wrote a note indicating my decline and signed it.

I declined because I had once been invited by the Kwa Zulu Police to help in an investigation where their member of parliament was murdered in Kwa Mashu. I was given some detectives and members seconded from what was known as the B51 to assist me with the investigation. This was regarded as the Security Branch of the Kwa Zulu Government. At the time of the investigation, there were some rivalries between some Inkatha warlords in the Ntuzuma and Inanda townships. There were sporadic attacks on each other by the Inkatha leaders.

One afternoon I was with the officer in charge of the B51 members in his office. There was a report that the warlord of Inanda Pisang had attacked Lindelani, which was under the late Shabalala. At the time of the alleged attack, Shabalala was said to be away in Ladysmith. The officer in charge of the B51, a man who was very well known to me, and who I considered a friend, picked up the phone and made a call.

I picked up from the conversation that he was speaking to the Commissioner of the Kwa Zulu Police. It went like this: "Sir, I have had enough of the Ponds. You know, sir, he went and attacked Shabalala's area while Shabalala was away. I am pleading for your help sir. I would like you to authorize me to open the armoury and dish out guns to a selected team of people, to go and sort him out once and for all."

It appeared that his ambitions were punctured flat, because when he hung up his bravado had melted. He ended by saying, "I will see what I can do."

I thought to myself, 'Well, here I am to help these detectives in a serious murder case of a prominent Kwa Zulu Government Member of Parliament. While that murder has got its own controversies, a senior officer in charge of a specialized branch of the Kwa Zulu police pleads for authorization to unleash a mass murder on an Inkatha stronghold. So if the officer in charge is ordering it, who was going to investigate it?'

The other person was a leader in his own right, representing an Inkatha constituency. I had good friends within the Kwa Zulu Police with who we had mutual respect on the basis of our capabilities in law enforcement. In our private conversations, they had expressed their desire for me to join them on the Kwa Zulu Police Force.

*****

When I returned to my station, a delegation of three senior Kwa Zulu Police officers visited me in my office in Pinetown. They said that they had been sent by their own head of detectives to talk me into joining them. There were promises of promotions in the offing.

I told them that my long-held principle was that there were to be no sacred cows in the journey of my career. For instance, I would want to be loyal to the people, the police and the government. I would not allow political warlords and corrupt high-ranking officers to interfere with my police work. I would have nothing to do with that kind of policing. I was fighting the same battles in the South African Police, and at least they were beginning to understand me there.

The delegation said that was the reason they wanted me so much to be part of them. They said I could strengthen those who were dedicated to police work, to be true servants of the people. There were many of them and they only wanted to strengthen the culture that I had mentioned. We parted on a cordial note. I felt that they were sincere in their purpose. I promised to think it over.

When Kwa Ndebele Police arrested Imbokodo members in Kwa Ndebele, even if it was for murder, if it concerned a victim other than Imbokodo members, they would order the suspect to be released immediately, and it was done.

After the meeting with the delegation from Ulundi, one of the members, a captain, was temporarily transferred to Mpumalanga. He had once been stationed at Nquthu, and was involved in the case of Inkosi Molefe. He was well-known as a skilful, hard worker, and highly experienced. He phoned to say he wanted to see me urgently. I invited him to Mpumalanga Training College where my wife worked as a matron, and had her quarters on the campus. Sometimes I visited her there.

He arrived very worried, and told me of the most amazing thing that had happened to him one evening at the Hammarsdale Police station. He said that when he got to Mpumalanga, he was handed several murder cases to investigate. He started working on the cases. On the evening in question, he was on duty at the evening police parade at the Hammarsdale Police Station. He said that there had been police, as well as Inkatha members of Mpumalanga Township on parade. The white police sergeant in charge of the parade discussed their targets for the night openly with the combined Inkatha and police members. There were discussions about which UDF houses to attack, and how and where they were situated.

After that parade, he decided to come and discuss that experience with me. He said that perhaps all the murder dockets he was supposed to investigate could have happened after such planning with police involvement. Was he expected, the following morning, to investigate murders which were planned in his presence? That, he said, was never going to happen. He thought that the people who had seen him during that parade perhaps thought that he was a cover-up specialist. He was not, and would show them by having nothing to do with the whole thing.

A few days after that meeting, he left Mpumalanga and Hammarsdale. I never heard from him or of him, until I heard that he had passed away some years later. Unfortunately or fortunately, however, I was not done with Kwa Ndebele. If you thought so, you were jumping the gun. As the Americans say: "You ain't seen nothing yet."

*****

When I returned home I received a letter of praise from the Commissioner's Office in Pretoria. It said that I had done my work with excellence. When we returned the dockets to Pretoria, it was in such haste, as if we were running away from a gathering storm. Piet Ntuli was not the only suspect for whom there was witness evidence.

We could still pursue criminal cases against Imokodo members, who, according to evidence in our possession, could be successfully prosecuted. It was also interesting that if I had been regarded as capable enough to be assigned to investigate the Kwa Ndebele government, it was strange and made no sense that I was removed from investigating the murder of one person, who happened to be Piet Ntuli.

It seemed to me that the whole plan was designed for me to identify through evidence, a person for whom they needed a reason to kill or remove from society. It was fashionable language, used by those who had embarked on their own final solution.

Piet Ntuli's death was never investigated.

PART 4

Professionalism, Good Hearts & Apartheid

Chapter 31
I need some answers

Some of the puzzles I came across, I have been able to anneals and untangle. I may have two of those to explain and clear if time allows. For now, I would like to deal with this one. The aspect of it that may not taste so good is that, although it is very interesting, the characters that feature in it shall have their names protected (for obvious reasons).

Most of this book is characterized by fear to hurt some people, although at times you will observe that some of these people deserve to be exposed and face the consequences of their actions. Though it is said that the truth will set people free, sometimes you want to save some people from being hurt. The sad part is when it hurts those close to the people who have been exposed. It is nice, though, when the writer knows that those concerned will know who they are because they alone will have to deal with their inner conscience. It will be left to them to tell others that what is being said is about them.

Back in 1979, I was involved in an investigation where a suspected murderer (a British citizen) allegedly killed his mistress, took some of her possessions, and gave them to other women. One woman who received the possessions is the subjects of this chapter.

I obtained a statement from her to the effect that she had never been presented with a sewing machine by the murder suspect. He was white and she was black. She was first apprehensive and she was worried about giving evidence in court against the murder suspect for the gifts. At any rate, she made the statement and was called to give evidence in court.

I had said before that, sometimes where apartheid and politics were concerned and where I knew that certain people would be victimized by the Security Branch on the grounds that they challenged apartheid, I did not feel guilty warning them.

In this case, one of my informers, a taxi owner, who focused on cases of theft of motor vehicles especially taxis, came to me one late afternoon during the mid-eighties and handed a photo album to me. He added that it was of people who called at his residence in Cleremont Township and left their luggage saying they would be taking a walk and would return later. As he handed me the album, he was very excited and seemed to feel that he was on to something very important. He went on to say that the people were from Transkei and, as far as he could infer, they were on their way to exile. He was certain that they were activists.

As far as I was concerned, and from what I had heard and had been observing, those people could be trapped at his home, arrested or kidnapped and taken to some far away farm, tortured, killed and buried there with their relatives and comrades thinking that they were in exile. I raced to Sangro House in Durban where I spoke to a relative of mine who was an advocate. He, in turn, got hold of a member of the UDF executive in KwaZaulu Natal to whom he took the photos and later returned them as I had emphasized that they be returned by all means. My purpose was to save those people but the photos had to be returned because the informer was likely to pass the information to, who unbeknown to me, his handlers at the Security Branch. I learnt, with great relief, that the people in the photos had been identified and, by any luck, would be saved.

I took the album back to the office with me. One of the people (a female) had an injury on one of her eyes (a kind of blue eye injury) as if she had been struck with a fist.

As soon as I got to my office the following morning, the first person to enter was a black Security Branch detective warrant officer. He was shaking with rage, and though we had treated one another with respect on many occasions, this time that would have been a luxury fit for the dust bin. His verbal rant was, "You know I have always respected you as a policeman and did not for any moment imagine that you hated us so much". Before I could say anything, he went on, "Please just hand over the photos and keep your explanations for another day if you have any".

I pulled the drawer on my desk in front of me, fished for the envelope with the photos and handed it over. He banged the door as he stepped out. I stood there as the shock melted, slowly weighing a few options in case his masters response became as drastic as ordering my detention to later charge me with treason.

To my surprise, nobody approached me to account for the kind of action I had undertaken. I found relief in the thought that perhaps they felt my only fault was that I kept the photos in my office instead of passing them on to them immediately. I kept telling myself that if they knew what I had done with the photos I would have long been dealt with in the manner they usually dealt with enemies of the apartheid state. If there was something called 'waving a red rag in front of a Spanish bull', I thought that was it.

*****

I need some answers, though, as goes the title of this chapter.

Some six months after the photo album episode, I received a visit from the same detective warrant officer of the Security Branch who had fetched the album. This time he was driven by a different urgency. He said he had been sent by his office to come and alert me of a serious threat to my life. As I listened to him, I thought to myself, 'Here we go again! What on earth would he be up to this time?'. However, I nodded my head to indicate 'I was listening'. Even though he had been subjected to sessions of rehearsals about how to put this thing to me, he appeared to be a lousy actor.

He said, "What I have come to warn you about is something that will be left entirely to you to deal with". I still nodded, with a stiff neck though. I was beginning to be annoyed because I was failing to imagine how naïve he thought I was. I was getting a bit unsettled because, under normal circumstances, I would be starting to read his mind and find answers. I thought to myself, 'Let me be patient and listen'.

He continued to say, "In a small shack built with cement blocks in front of the Cleremont Funeral Parlour, there are terrorists who had taken occupation for the duration of an operation they have been sent to undertake by the ANC in exile. Their mission is to eliminate you." He added that, "They have come from Mozambique for that purpose only." I asked him what the Security Branch expected me to do about it? His response was, "As I have said, we only have this information and it is up to you to do whatever you wanted with it seeing that you are also a policeman with powers."

If I thought in the beginning that he was only naïve, this time I was convinced that, not only was he a dimwit, but a thoroughly brain-washed nincompoop.

First, it was a guarded secret of the Security Branch on how terrorists moved and what they were up to in the country. What they did was also part of their dark secrets. If we detectives were ever found displaying interest in political activists, let alone terrorists, we would be reigned in to account for such interest.

Second, now they knew of a house where armed terrorists were and which terrorists were on a mission to kill a policeman. Instead of doing what they always did under such circumstances, for the first time in known history, they were delegating that duty to ordinary me!

These were thoughts running in my head, not what I was saying to him.

After listening to him stutter all that drivel, I asked him if he knew why the terrorists wanted to kill me. He said that they had been sent by a woman whom I had obtained a statement from and had humiliated by getting her to go to court to testify that a white man who had killed his mistress had presented her with a sewing machine which was part of the belongings of the woman who had been.

I stayed away from putting pointed questions to him because I thought it wiser that way. I did not want his masters to know that I was aware of what they were up to. I said to him, "Thank you very much for the information" I told him that I think it over and resolve the best course of action.

He responded that I should not take too long. I thanked him and left.

As he left, my thoughts went back to the photos and back to the fact tha,t in 1980, the Security Branch had invited me to join them but I had politely turned them down. They were the ones who had the experience of dealing with terrorists and they knew that I had none, and that I had zero capacity to handle such situations.

I decided to approach my branch commander at Pinetown at the time. When I entered his office, it seemed as if he expected me and that he was even aware of what the call was about, although I cannot explain why I felt that way.

I sat down without him indicating that I should do so. I had this feeling that what I was going to tell him could not be said while standing.

He said, "What is it sergeant?" I told him that I had something to report, "Go ahead I'm listening" he said.

I told him that I had come to report something very strange. I went on to inform him that a detective had approached me from the Security Branch to warn me that there were terrorists in the country all the way from Mozambique on a mission to kill me. The alleged reason was that I had taken a statement from and sent a subpoena to a woman from Cleremont Township to give evidence in court because a white man who killed his mistress and took her possessions had given a sewing machine to the woman from Cleremont. According to the Security Branch, by so doing, the woman felt that I had humiliated her and, as such, deserved to die in the hands of terrorists.

My branch commander, an English speaking white man just past his middle age, listened with neither emotion nor interest. He appeared too casual for someone hearing such a report.

I continued to say what puzzled me about the Security Branch information is that they were saying that it was up to me to handle the matter of the threat to my life by terrorists, the whereabouts of whom they knew.

He then said, "Is that all?" When I responded in the affirmative, he calmly and calculatingly said, "You see Sergeant, I am only an ordinary crime detective, not a special or security branch member and definitely not a politician. If you (nodding his head towards me) and the Security Branch policemen, who deal with political matters and the terrorists who are a military arm of politicians, have come to a point where you want to kill each other, you must please understand that, that is way, way out of my line. I do not involve myself in those matters and that is not an area I am trained to deal with, I suggest you report that matter to the Security Branch".

I was so shocked; I could not believe that he just said those things. For instance, I could not go to the Special Branch to report a matter which they felt, for reasons of their, should be reported to me. Nor could I approach the said terrorists at the address given and present myself to them. I could not even approach the person who was alleged to have brought them from Mozambique to come and kill me. I was convinced that the whole thing was a set up. I felt it was another way of forcing me to join the Security Branch. I also felt that they were or would be monitoring my movements such that, if I decided to attack the said terrorists with a view of arresting them, I would be forced to either kill or be killed.

If I killed, the Security Branch would pretend to arrest me only to pretend to rescue me from the case on condition that I joined them. Because terrorists would have been killed, they (the Security Branch) would automatically handle the case and only they would know everything. That way, I would automatically fall under the killing squad of the Security Branch and be ruined as a policeman or even a person. So, I did nothing.

However, that was not the end of that game; the worst was still to come.

Two months down the line, I was in my office one morning when a black major in the Security Branch whom I happened to know very well came to my office and asked if he could speak to me in his car, parked in the street, alongside our station building on Old Main Road, Pinetown. I followed him to his Volkswagen, which had two passengers in the back seat. They were two elderly and very thin, a man and a woman, and very much Transkeian rural peasant types.

I got into the passenger seat while the major got into the driver's seat and immediately got down to introductions. He told me that the two were man and wife and they were from Transkei and were relatives of the woman who allegedly brought the terrorists for me. He first asked if I still remember the warning given to me by the warrant officer from the Security Branch about terrorists from Mozambique. When I said 'yes' he went on to say that he had brought witnesses who were at the meeting where the matter of killing me was discussed. He said they thought I needed further evidence before taking action.

At that point I 'washed my hands' off these people. Theirs was such a sick joke that, if it were not a deadly one, I would think it was an act from a parade of clowns competing for a number one spot award in the confused world of lunacy.

The show in the car took its own theatrical level of a bizarre act when the woman started crying, rather uncontrollably, until her 'husband' comforted her on his chest like a crying baby while the major and I looked in complete disbelief and I thought what would happen if the major was not part of the act.

When the woman's crying act subsided, in between sobs, she spoke as some black women would do when preaching or praying, "I am crying because it is the first time in my life that I am in a car and so close to a person I happen to know will be dead anytime". She continued, "When the discussion about killing you took place in our presence in Cleremont, being led by our own daughter, because she is my sister's daughter who since passed away, it never occurred to me that they were talking about a dignified and innocent looking person like yourself. It now dawns on me how people can be cruel. We warned against it even though we did not have the picture of the person you are".

The major said, "We thought we should bring these people to you so that you know that there are witnesses in this matter".

Failing to understand the whole thing was just about killing me, I just said, "Thank you for everything." I still did not say what I was going to do.

For the Security Branch, there was a ready-made case with

suspected terrorists who allegedly had AK47 rifles with them in an identified room. Two witnesses who attended a meeting where planning of killing a policeman was being discussed, the person who had been behind the plan was well known and available in Cleremont Township, with the motive having also been confirmed by the would be victim. I am still wondering and still more than eager to know, what it was all about.

Perhaps some of the characters involved after reading this book will be visited by their conscience and decide to free me from this that still denies confirmation to me; so that we, at long last, are truly free. I sometimes felt I should have taken the matter to the TRC, but I felt I would be abusing the process if I expected the TRC to deal with my personal issues because I was part of it.

Editors Note: *we have no idea whether the author finally found an answer to this puzzle before he joined the heavens. We hope that, despite the passage of time, the answer will be forthcoming, a matter that would assure a peaceful rest of his departed soul.*

Chapter 32
My Tool to Tilt the Granite Wall

There were times when I forced white officers to recognize and respect me as an accomplished professional. I did my work in such a way that it became difficult for them to ignore me. On the whole, I feel that many I did helped the cause of policing. This is supported by the fact that judges of the Supreme Court and magistrates made glowing compliments of how I conducted my investigations, and presented my cases before them. They also commented that my kind of performance would only make the South African Police Force proud. They added that would go a long way to assure members of the public of high standards of service from the police.

Even if some high-ranking officers did not have a particular liking for me, for whatever reason, they would only find themselves in a quandary. If they claimed to be loyal to the police force, and the country, harbouring negative feelings about me would only show how misguided they were.

What we learnt and understood about the white people, who spoke Afrikaans, was that they were straightforward when it came to demonstrating their preferences for and objections to ideas, actions or even people. Some of them would develop friendships with certain black people and would show complete trust and confidence in the ability and capability of their black friends, servants or partners in whatever enterprise that would have brought them together.

There was a white Afrikaans captain who I worked with in a crime-prevention unit in Pinetown. He was a known racist, aggressive and totally unfriendly, according to black detectives who worked with him. Other black detectives and some whites were puzzled by the way he showed respect for me.

He was in charge of our unit, which was very successful in its crime prevention drive. I played a kind of leadership role, in that I was the one with a the widest informer network in the team. As a result, I became a major source of information in the unit for planning strategies to confront crime in our area. Of course, as head of the unit, its successes were attributed to the captain's leadership.

As indicated, when Afrikaners appreciated a black person, they did not show it in half measures. If the black person spoke Afrikaans fluently, it was a cherry on top for their cake of the friendship. My captain seemed to entertain that kind of attachment to me.

One day he demonstrated that by inviting me to his house. He introduced me to his wife in English, perhaps so that I could hear him say, "This is detective Sergeant Magadhla, the only black man I have ever invited into my house. This is the only black policeman of whom I will not be ashamed to have a beer and dinner in my house. He is far different from the other blacks I know."

His wife stood there, not knowing what to do. What do people do when they are being introduced in that manner? I did not know either. I just stood there, waiting for his next word. I was ushered onto a sofa and we had dinner and beer together. That seemed to me one of those aspects of apartheid which imprisoned white people. Their guilt was a good reason to extricate themselves from the huge burden which was placed on us in South Africa; the burden of apartheid.

Our common humanity should have been like a magnet that drew us all into a family of happy people, to confront together the ills along the way. Instead of being able to laugh and cry, to prosper and rejoice together, we allowed ourselves to be prisoners of ideology and puppets of perceptions.

Chapter 33
Sergeant Bartels

He was one of my true white friends. He was a detective colleague at Hillcrest police station during the late seventies. He was of German descent, but spoke English, Afrikaans and Zulu fluently. He played rugby and cricket well. Most of the time we worked together in our detective duties.

He was a diligent and skilful detective. Apartheid and the colour of our skins mattered little to us. We were simply colleagues and good friends. He hated the fact that he earned more money than I did; yet we were doing the same job. We were exposed to the same dangers and demands at work. We solved very interesting cases together. He would resist attempts from any racist superior who tried to set us apart on the grounds of his being too close to me in a manner that apartheid did not favour.

We have remained close friends right up to the present. We defied apartheid together and did things our way. I appreciated his courage, because under apartheid, he, as a white person, had to be courageous to maintain an open friendship with a black person. He was one of those whites who were beacons of light in the dark days of apartheid.

Chapter 34
Captain Dutton and I

We met at Pinetown Police station during the mid-eighties when he was a warrant officer. We worked in the detective Branch Field or Crime Prevention Unit. Some of us carried and investigated dockets while others collected information and conducted crime raids, recovered exhibits and charged those responsible.

When we first started, we concentrated on robberies, house breaking-ins and thefts. We later took on murders, rapes and other more serious cases. These included arson and politically influenced murders. Ours became a very successful crime unit in the Durban West Police District. There were senior and junior white and black detectives in the unit. There was a sprinkle of uniform members whom we had drawn into our unit because of their diligence and alertness. There was harmony and unity in the unit. When Warrant Officer Frank Dutton was promoted to the rank of Lieutenant, he took charge of the unit.

We formed a cordial working partnership. I held the rank of a Detective Sergeant at the time. Racism played no part in our working relationship. We both worked towards the goal of achieving unity in our team, irrespective of the colour of one's skin. Focus on our work and respect for each other and other members of the public we served, was uppermost in the unit. Most of the successes we achieved in our work cemented the cordial working relationship between Detective Warrant Officer Frank Dutton and me. He was senior by rank to all the members and I was regarded senior by age and service to all the black members of the unit. Our time always working and travelling together drew us to taking note of the racism and the discriminatory practices around us. As a white person, he chose to shun racist practices, although they were meant to cushion his life better than mine. What developed into a friendship and a brotherhood between us, while being colleagues at work, set us free from man-made indiscretions and pitfalls that clouded some of us from concentrating on what our oath of office demanded from us -- protecting lives, and preventing and investigating crime.

There were times when I was subjected to humiliation by white racist policemen when we were together. He did not need to apologize because he knew that he was not party to it. I remember one day when we called at Brits Police Station in the North West Province to make enquires in connection with an investigation we were conducting. When a white male sergeant came out of the charge office to greet Captain Dutton, my colleague introduced himself and me. He then extended his hand to shake hands with the sergeant. I, too, because I had been introduced, extended my own hand towards the sergeant who quickly withdrew his hand, leaving mine was hanging in the air. However, it was not the first time something like that had happened to me. We had become used to it. Sometimes they would offer him tea or coffee and invite him inside while I would wait outside. He would politely find an excuse such as he was all right; but I knew he was doing it for my sake.

It would have been awkward for him and I travelling long distances together discussing everything normal people discussed only for him to be isolated from me for special treatment in some corner while he knew I was thirsty too. We did everything we could on equal terms except that I always kept in mind that he was senior to me in rank and I accorded him the respect that went with that. We were in apartheid South Africa and in an apartheid Police Force. Our kind of a free relationship worried some of our colleagues sympathetic to apartheid. Some intimated that it was because he was English-speaking and vulnerable to my manipulation. They were wrong because we needed no manipulation to regard each other as normal people, made different by skin pigmentation. I would not have bothered if he voted for the National Party or any other white party. In fact, we did not even discuss that. It seemed we were both careful that our political leanings did not interfere with our police work. Most of the apartheid sympathizers in the police force could have been members of the National Party for all I knew. Whatever they did or felt about me did not matter and I was in no way trying to seek favour from the ANC which they were brought up to fear as a communist terrorist monster.

Many a time Dutton demonstrated that he was not a racist and that caused him to be shunned by racists in the force. We once took a long a trip to Port Elizabeth in the Eastern Cape to pick up a witness. On the way, as we realized that it was getting towards sunset, we stopped at police stations to try and arrange a place to sleep. At two of the police stations we approached we were told that there would be accommodation for him only and not for me. They suggested that because the police stations were in areas designated 'whites only',

I could only get accommodation in the police stations in the black townships. Captain Dutton did not accept that arrangement and we carried on until we reached Port Elizabeth and went straight to Le Grange Police Station, a new police station in Port Elizabeth at the time. It had new detention facilities for political activists.

When we got to the charge office, Captain Dutton reported about our mission and also the fact that we were in need of accommodation. He was told that the new police station barracks offered something like a five-star hotel but for whites only and that, as far as that was concerned, his problem was solved. As for me, t the only place I could be accommodated was outside in the township black police station barracks or else if there were still black detective members at the police station they could take me to their houses. They had all left and while my case was still to be decided. Captain Dutton spoke to a young white constable asking him to show us around the police station. The two of us were led on a tour of the station. When we got to the political detention cells, we marvelled at the beauty and cleanliness of the place. The cells for whites even had beds with white sheets.

Captain Dutton told the constable that he would not return to the charge office but would solve our accommodation problem by putting up there. There were even facilities for making coffee or tea in the cells. We went to purchase food from a nearby tearoom and slept in the cells for the night. We expected controversy about it; strangely, we were not challenged about it.

We got our witness and home we drove back. All the other racist station commanders along the way and in Port Elizabeth did not even seem to realize how much I was being hurt by their attitudes. It also did occur to me that, for the extremist racists, seeing that I felt hurt derived the satisfaction they desired.

*****

While working from our Pinetown office we received a report that some members of our team were involving themselves in politically influenced crimes such as forming themselves into groups over weekends and patrolling areas dominated by comrades (UDF youth activists.) The purpose, so it was said, of these patrols was to enforce a curfew where no comrades were to be seen on the streets or anywhere away from their homes from starting 9 p.m. These policemen would move around with heavily armed Inkatha vigilantes.

When reports were made to us about these police unlawful activities, we called them in for questioning. However, they said that they were aware that even if we were to pursue cases against them, intimidation would get the better of whoever would be a witness.

We warned them and we continued with our work but kept a keen eye on the issue. This was taking place in the St. Wendoline area of Marrianhill or Pinetown. It so happened that the vigilantes involved from time to time held kangaroo court trials where they tried their own members and those of the public who fell into their hands.

On this particular day, they tried one of their civilian members for allegedly handing over ammunition to his sister who was in love with a comrade and who in turn handed the ammunition to the comrade. At the 'trial', which was on the veranda of a house among the shacks of St. Wendoline, it was alleged that the accused civilian member was given a break when one of the members of the kangaroo court went to smoke and stretch. He (the accused) went to his cousin's shack and gave him a piece of paper and pen and asked him to write a list of people they had killed during their terror activities in the form of vigilantes in St. Wendoline right up to Nongoma in Zulu land. He told his cousin that he was almost certain that his accusers would find him guilty and sentence him to death.

Soon after he returned for the resumption of his 'trial', gun shots were heard and the 'accused' was found lying dead on the veranda.

His cousin brought the list of revelations to me. I got a team of good investigators and we followed the matter up. Some of the names on the list of murders, including the one at Nongoma, were vigilantes who were also hired to eliminate individuals alleged to be witches. We arrested the vigilantes including two of our own members who happened to be those we had previously warned to stop involvement in vigilantism, especially where political rivalry was at stake.

When the police members were charged and one of them convicted, Captain Dutton and I had a surprise invitation to call at the local headquarters where a brigadier of the Security Branch addressed us. It was obviously difficult for him to say what he wanted to say, except for saying that the policeman we had got convicted was a good policeman and was doing a good job. We wondered what he wanted us to do about it because, as far as we were concerned, there had been enough evidence to prove the policeman guilty of criminality. How any of that was a good job by the policeman was baffling, to say the least.

What was clear to me about that was that the brigadier was a member of the rogue element ,or third force if you like. He had all the power to act against us if we had broken the law, but because he knew he was the one acting against the law, he was left helpless. That little act of his encouraged me and gave me credit in the eyers of the majority of the members of the South African Police, black and white, who did not taint themselves with the brush of serving apartheid against the South African people.

*****

Based on all the information Dutton and I gathered, it was easy to confirm the existence of the Third Force and the allied violence in South Africa especially in KwaZulu Natal. We found a Judge and reported the matter to him. After submitting our report to the Honourable Judge, a whole lot of positive actions influenced the country's political scene, especially on the security front. It had such an effect it only needed a De Klerk[1], who had just emerged victorious from the last whites-only referendum and a Mandela who had just emerged from Robben Island as star, to create an epitome of peace for the country.

When we eventually got to where we are today in world ratings, I for one, as insignificant in matters of intellect and scholastic profile, harbour a living desire that the honourable judge, to whom Captain Dutton and I reported the activities of the Third Force, be recognized by South Africa and the world for his contribution in changing the direction of our beloved country from the cloak and dagger journey of calamity and doom. Now that everybody's medals have been presented and citations are out, it would be most fitting for his family to enjoy his.

This brings me to where I say without fear or favour that De Klerk deserved the Nobel Prize along with Mandela. Having seen what I saw in the apartheid police force during its lifetime, I do not find any reason to doubt that some of the things that were done by members of the force, he in fact did not know. I am also saying that, after he got to know about them and took the kind of action he did at the time, nobody doubted his sincerity. Generals in the police force and the army were suspended, some dismissed and investigated, which was the first of its kind with any of the National Party presidents or

---

1 **Editor's Note:** on his deathbed, former South African president, De Klerk, through a recorded message apologized profusely for having been part of the oppressive system of apartheid; he wished that those who had suffered under the rule of the abhorrent regime could forgive him and his peers that perpetuated the oppression.

prime ministers. I am almost sure that whatever action he took in response to the knowledge he had received, he did not do so with the Nobel Prize in mind. What he was almost certain of was that the action he took would, in the final analysis, not be in favour of the National Party, nor was it out of his love for the ANC.

PART 5
Despair versus Hope

CHAPTER 35
Candles of Hope

In the midst of misery and the darkest hour in the history of South Africa, there were those individuals who, on their own volition, torchbearers of hope. This was despite the prospect of being labelled and castigated, sneered at and isolated. I am sure that it was a result of their upbringing, and their natural compassion towards all of the family of humankind.

They sought neither fame nor favour for what they did. The visitation of the spirit of kindness and warmth in their souls filtered through all those in their presence and beyond. They touched the hearts that yearned for love and peace.

Along my journey through the police establishment during apartheid, I had occasion to associate and work with wonderful Afrikaans-speaking senior police officers. I take the liberty of mentioning their names in this book, despite having tried and failed to solicit their consent. I believe in harmless truth, clean and clear of any malice, but flowing from my reservoir of appreciation for their uprightness, and devotion to police work which I saw in them. I saw only goodness in them. I am also driven by the fact that the circumstances prevailing at the time were not favourable or enabling for me to have expressed myself the way I do now. I can express now how I felt when they courageously became who they were, irrespective of the norm having been the opposite.

To me they were candles of hope. They were the people who made it happen for me in terms of moulding, supporting, and sharpening my investigative skills.

Detective Sergeant Busuidenhout

Detective Sergeant Busuidenhout of Mayville Police Station, who actually discovered me as a prospect and gave me the mentorship and protection is the one I owe for my entry into the second level of what became an eventful career for me. First was my entry into the South African Police Force as a uniformed policeman.

Mayville Police Station was one of the newly-built police stations during in the nineteen 1950s. During that time there was no murder and robbery unit for Durban. Whenever there was a serious case in Durban and surrounding areas involving murders and robberies, a special unit of selected detectives was put together to conduct the investigations. From my vantage point, those were detectives of special talent and courage. They used to detain their suspects in the new police cells in Mayville. When these detectives came to interrogate their suspects, for some reason, they took to a liking for me and used to invite me to sit with them and listen. I made it a point to really sharpen my ears and observe. It took a short time before they allowed me to ask the suspects being interviewed questions of my own.

Sergeant Busuidenhout, who spoke Zulu very fluently and beautifully, used to join in also. He was Acting Detective Branch Commander at Mayville at the time. I was working in the enquiries section in the uniformed branch. One day, while the murder and robbery detectives were interrogating suspects, Detective Busuidenhout was listening to my participation. He invited me to his office and asked me if I would like to be a detective. When I said 'Yes', he asked me to apply to join the detective branch, which I did, and he attached his own recommendation and put in his brief supporting me and off he went to the Durban West District Headquarters. Upon his return that very same afternoon, he gave me the good news that the following morning I should report to his office to start as a probationer detective. He took it upon himself to give me the best guidance possible. I did not disappoint him. The attempted murder docket he assigned to me to investigate came back from court with a commendation from a regional court magistrate.

What made Sergeant Busuidenhout so elated with the magistrate's remarks, about how well the case was investigated, was that I had followed his instructions to the letter. He was instructed to escort me to the office of the District Crime Detective Office at the Headquarters to convey the thanks from the regional magistrate personally. That also said a lot about him as a mentor. It enhanced his own status.

One day, he did the most amazing thing for me. He demonstrated his trust in me in a manner that left me in disbelief and great puzzlement. He called me into his office and asked me to lock the door behind me. He told me that he had no doubt about my determination to become a good detective and most of all about my loyalty. However what he was going to tell me depended on how I would handle it, but as for him he would be with me all the way.

As I listened with bated breath, I felt that I was sweating. He said that he had called me to alert me that the clerk of the station commander of Cato Manor Police Station, where our barracks was, had written a long report to the Security Branch about my activities at the police barracks.

He reported that I was influencing black policemen to be aware of political developments in Ghana and Congo and their respective leaders, Dr. Kwame Nkrumah and Patrice Lumumba. The report also alleged that I encouraged a civilian to open an assault case against a policeman who was subsequently convicted for the case. The clerk also reported that I was the one behind the demand that we manage our police mess in the barracks, which we eventually won, and I became the Mess Committee Chairman.

Indeed, I had read newspapers at the barracks and discussed them with my friends and of course I encouraged a civilian to report the unlawful assault by the policeman.

Given that the matter had been written in confidence, it was a very serious matter for the sergeant to confide in me. I knew that his loyalty was to the government of South Africa, its constitution and its people, but not to the whims of apartheid.

When my branch commander came across the report from the Security Branch, he called me to his office and gushed his heart out, demonizing me as a communist agent planted within the police force. What made him see red was that 'I had made a fool of him', by presenting myself to him as trustworthy, causing him to share confidential things, which he otherwise would not have, had he known my true colours. He spent six months not talking to me. He eventually had to when a letter of commendation came from the court, instructing him to escort me to the District Headquarters for the District Head of detectives to thank me on behalf of the court for a case which the court had said had been exceptionally well investigated

It was poetic justice watching him savour the praise he got for having a member like me in his staff. It placed his branch in good stead. Nothing became of the alleged report to the Security Branch.

Col. Venter

In 1979 when I was stationed in Pinetown, I was involved in the investigation of one Roy Peter Barber, a British citizen. He had come to South Africa with Mrs. Jones and her daughter, both of whom he had allegedly murdered in 1973 in Pinetown, and whose bodies were never found. Col. Venter, who was the District Crime Officer of Durban West, was in charge of the case. Because the three bodies in respect of which Barber was charged, had not been found right up to the time of the Supreme Court trial, investigations carried on while the trial proceeded.

When the investigation team met to discuss strategies before the court proceedings started, I suggested that I be allowed to go and check with the banks. I wanted to see if one of the women Barber allegedly murdered, and with whom he had occupied a flat in New Germany at the time of her disappearance, had a bank account in one of the banks in New Germany. I missed the court trial that morning to follow that angle of enquiry. Indeed, I found that she had an account with the Standard Bank and that, from around the time of her disappearance, her account was never serviced, and she had not responded even to correspondence informing her of her accrued interest.

All the efforts the bank made to contact her had been to no avail. That, in a way, reinforced the strong suspicion that she had died and that Barber had much to do with it. Her disappearance followed that of Mrs. Jones and her daughter. I returned to court around 12:30 p.m. and reported the matter to Colonel Venter. He immediately communicated the information to the State Counsel, who asked for the court to stand down, until the following Tuesday. That would allow time for someone to verify and link the account to her identity, which was to be confirmed by the Bantu Affairs Department in Pretoria.

When the court adjourned, Colonel Venter invited me to his office at the District Headquarters. It was on a Friday during lunchtime. It was the usual practice for officers to have a *braai* for lunch downstairs. I remained in his office while he went to join the others at the *braai*. He soon came back with two plates of meat and bread rolls, and we enjoyed lunch together. It is significant to mention this because that was not done at that time. It needed courage, even for a high-ranking officer, to break that norms. Colonel Venter said that the Supreme Court had adjourned until Tuesday because of my individual effort, and it would not make sense for everyone else to enjoy a good meal while I did not. He told me that he had broken the news of the breakthrough to the other officers at the *braai*, and they had contributed towards the meat and rolls for my plate.

That was not all for Colonel Venter; there was more to come for him to demonstrate his firm backbone under many difficult circumstances.

Still on the Roy Peter Barber case, I had to travel to Johannesburg to interview Mr. Crowther who had a love affair with Phillipine Ndlovu, the woman whose body had not been found. Mr. Crowther has previously worked in a factory in New Germany. I also planned to trace a black man from Brakpan, who Barber alleged had been the husband of Phillipine Ndlovu and whom Barber alleged had taken her to Johannesburg. A major from the headquarters, who was the colonel's deputy, offered to go with me to Johannesburg.

We wanted to inquire from Mr. Crowther if he had any idea about what happened to Phillipine Ndlovu. When the major and I found him, he first denied that he had any previous a love affair with Phillipine while he was working in New Germany. The major had told him that I was the one who would interview him and he (the major) was only accompanying me. When I produced some facts to counter his denials, Mr. Crowther admitted his affair with Phillipine. When I was ready to take a statement from him, he suggested that the statement be taken that evening because he had to go to work and would return in the evening. It was arranged that the major would take the statement later. When I parted with the major, I phoned the colonel to report to him that Crowther had agreed to make a statement about what he knew about Phillipine.

The following morning, the major and I planned to proceed to the Brakpan location to look for Phillipine's husband, as Barber alleged. When we got to fill up petrol at Brakpan Police Station, the major went inside to meet an old friend who was the Branch Commander of Detectives in Brakpan. Soon, the major returned in the company of the commander, who was also a Major in rank. He accused me of bringing the Major all the way from Natal for nothing. He said he had sent his men to the Brakpan location and they had not found any witnesses, and he had sent a letter to Durban to that effect. I told him that we received the letter but I wanted to go to Brakpan because my information was different and did not align with his report.

The major and I continued to the Brakpan location where I was informed that the alleged husband would be found in Lesly, Eastern Transvaal. Later, we found the witness, the alleged husband, Mr. Maseko, and took a statement from him. He denied knowing Phillipine's whereabouts.

When we got back to Durban and the colonel saw the statement Crowther had made, in which he was then denying his relationship with Phillipine, he (the colonel) decided to go to Johannesburg himself, to bring Crowther, so that I could interview him in his

The Colour of the Skunk

presence. When he returned with Crowther, the colonel convened an interview session with Crowther, in the presence of the whole team investigating the Roy Pieter Barbers' murders.

I was tasked with interviewing Crowther and we set the time for 9 p.m. in our office in Pinetown. There were five white senior detectives, including the colonel and the major. Then there was Crowther in the interview room.

The colonel addressed us saying that he had brought Crowther to be questioned in his presence, so that he would hear it from the horse's mouth, as it were, whatever it was. He said that he would like me to speak to Crowther in everybody's presence, so that none could claim to have heard otherwise.

I started from the same place when I first spoke to Crowther at his home in Johannesburg. Before midnight, we took a break to have tea. The major called out to an Indian sergeant who was on guard at the detectives' offices to make the tea. He shouted at him, saying, "Chockra make us some tea." I did not know what *chockra* meant. I thought it was something derogatory to the sergeant, but while writing this book, I did some research, only to find that it may have been used as a term of affection, as it meant 'son' or 'boy.' In any case, the sergeant did not seem to have taken offence. But again, would he have shown it if he did?

The sergeant brought six cups of tea to the table. As was the norm, he had counted the six white people around the table, including Crowther, brought six cups of tea, and placed one in front of each. I also did not feel as if there was something out of the ordinary about it. I had become used to my place under such circumstances.

It felt awkward for the major, though. Remember, this was the major who, when I was involved in a fraud investigation involving members of the firearm unit, and when we worked from his office at the headquarters, had their tea maker serve me tea from the officers' tea club. Although this, on its own, caused some of his colleagues to raise their eyebrows, he did it all the same. He had told me that if the others complained, he would add to his share of the contribution to the tea club in order to accommodate me. We used to have the tea in his office when I was there.

He did not go to join the others in the tearoom. He also had made it a point that my cup was not different from the others. I knew that he was risking ostracism or being called to explain, but it appeared he was ready for any such event. In the interview with Crowther, I sat next to him. He simply moved his cup of tea to me and remained with none. Then he called, "Chockra, where is my tea?" The sergeant came back and looked to find that there was no longer a teacup in front of the major. He appeared puzzled, even shocked and dumbstricken. He simply shook his head in disbelief, and went to fetch a cup of tea for the major. I had my tea with the team, including Crowther.

The atmosphere around the table was charged. While the two junior white officers present were battling to recover from the shock, the colonel and the major seemed to enjoy the moment. To me, a positive and historic statement had been made that night. To the two junior detectives around the table and the Sergeant Chockra, a homework assignment had been given to them by the events around that table at that moment.

Back to the interview.

Before her disappearance, Phillipine had been working at a service station in New Germany, serving petrol. She was one of the first black females doing that kind of work at that time. That was where Barber met her, and they fell in love.

It was during that time when Barber took leave from work where he ran a kitchen cupboards business. The work involved selling and installing cupboard fittings in households around New Germany, Pinetown, Durban and the surrounding areas. He had done fittings in Clermont Township and had made friends with some of the customers. One such friend was a taxi owner known as Mageba. Mageba knew Phillipine and about her affair with Barber. When Barber went on leave, he went along with Phillipine to Namibia, South West Africa at that time. He had rented a flat in New Germany and had got Phillipine to join him there, where they stayed together as a couple. Because he was so much in love with Phillipine, it seemed, he had pressure to get rid of the lady who was known as his wife, Mrs. Jones, and her daughter. He had lived with both of them in a house in Westville. He killed them both and then went to live with Phillipine.

Barber was known to be a very jealous and a violent lover. It happened that one day when Phillipine was in Clermont visiting friends, she stopped a taxi driven by Mageba, and asked for a lift to Pinetown. Mageba was Barber's friend. Barber had fitted kitchen cardboards in Mageba's kitchen.

Along the way, Phillipine asked Mageba to stop the taxi in front of a factory where an elderly white man was waiting. She joined the man who, it later turned out to be Crowther. He had worked at that factory before moving to Johannesburg. For some strange reason, Phillipine had a weakness or preference for men far older than she was, and in particular, old white men.

When Mageba left her with Crowther, he drove straight to Barber. He reported that he left his girlfriend with a man and that they had walked together into a factory, which he went and pointed out to Barber. It was reported that Barber tried to enter the factory through the only entrance, and the main gate where Mageba had dropped off Phillipine. The gate was locked with a large steel lock. Barber tried everything to enter, but could not manage. The gate was so tall that he could not climb over. He then went to a locksmith, purchased an even bigger lock, went back and locked the factory gate from outside while Crowther and Phillipine were inside. Later in the evening, when Crowther and Phillipine got to the gate, they found that they had been locked in with a lock for which they had no key.

It was clear that Barber had felt that, because he had failed to enter the gate because he had no key to open the lock, he had better 'feed them with their own medicine', as it were. They would find the gate locked with a lock for which the had no key. They would then feel the pain of being unable to get out as had been the case with him when he was trying to get in. It was clearly another indication of Barber's aggression.

When I related this scenario at Crowther's interview, I told him that in my subsequent investigation about that particular incidence, I went to a locksmith and got all the details about Barber's purchasing the lock and locking him (Crowther) inside the factory. He gave up and admitted that indeed he had had a love affair with Phillipine. He went on to say that he had lately been seeing newspaper reports about a search being made for Phillipine. He had written a letter to one of Phillipine's friends and tried to find out from her if she knew of Phillipine's whereabouts, but had not received a reply. He gave the friend's address in the Maphumulo District, via Stanger.

It was at this point, after midnight, that Crowther declared that he was prepared to swear an affidavit about all he knew about Phillipine and Barber. At this point, the colonel announced that the interview would end there, because he had gotten all that was needed. He offered to take Crowther to his hotel and would fetch him in the morning to go to his office to obtain the affidavit. He asked me to meet him in his office, so that after he had taken the affidavit, we would then drive to Stanger and Maphumulo. We were going to trace the letter that Crowther had said he had written to Phillipine's friend about her whereabouts.

The following morning I drove to the colonel's office at the Durban West Detective headquarters. He had just finished taking Crowther's statement and he handed it over to me too read. When I finished reading it, he asked me if I was happy with it; if so, he would drive Crowther to the airport to fly back to Johannesburg. When I said I was happy, the colonel asked me to wait for him while he took Crowther to the airport.

The colonel returned from the airport, we got into his car, and drove to Stanger. Then in what was supposed to make me happy, but got me scared, the colonel in his own joy and happiness for me, dropped a bombshell which was the reason for him to cherish and embrace that little moment in the car. He said, "Sergeant you cannot imagine the importance of what you have done for South Africa today." I remained silent and worried, because, however swiftly I tried to run my mind on what he was about to reveal, it was as evasive as a flea. I just became a sitting duck for his bomb. He went on to say, "You have been an ambassador for South Africa." I still waited with bated breath. "Let me start the story from the beginning," he said and continued, "When I was taking Crowther to the airport, by the way, Crowther is a citizen of New Zealand.... he told me that after what happened to him these past few days, he feels duty-bound to take leave and go back home to New Zealand, because of the good news he had for them and the world.

Crowther's story went like this: He was at his home in Johannesburg, when three people arrived. One was a white senior detective officer with his brother-in-law. They had a black man with them, whom they introduced to him as the detective who was to speak to him about the matter they were investigating. He had tried to deny the facts put to him by the black detective, who later convinced him, and he decided to tell him the truth. When he suggested that an affidavit was to be made, he (Crowther) had suggested that he had to go in the afternoon and would be available in the evening for the affidavit. The white detective officer offered to come back in the evening to obtain the affidavit. The black detective agreed and they all left. In the evening, the white officer and his brother-in-law came, and after they had supper and some drinks, then started with the statement. In the absence of the black detective, and the relaxing influence of the liquor, he had seen a chance to change his statement back to the denial he first attempted when questioned by the black detective. The white officer had then taken the affidavit in its denial form. Crowther had thought everything was fine, only to be shocked by the arrival of the colonel at his home to fetch him and take him all the way to the black detective, to whom he had verbally made a statement admitting his affair with Phillipine.

When he got to Durban, a night interview was arranged. In that interview, the colonel had told the team of white detectives that he had brought him (Crowther) so that the black detective could interview him and that the other detectives would just listen. He went on to mention the tea incidence where the Indian sergeant had not given a cup of tea to the black detective to whom he had made a verbal statement at his home in Johannesburg, but to the white detective officers only. Thereupon, the white officer who had been with the white detective officer at his home, shouted to the Indian sergeant for his tea, which he had pushed to the black detective. Then when he had gone back to the statement he had made to the black detective in Johannesburg, the colonel offered to take him back to his hotel in Durban and then to his office, where the colonel took the affidavit himself. When the black detective arrived, he handed it to him to read and to approve. When the black detective read the statement, the colonel asked him if he was happy with it. The black detective said that he was. The colonel took him to the airport to fly back to Johannesburg.

The gist of what was being said, according to the colonel, was that Crowther was saying when he got back to his country, New Zealand, he was going to go to a member of parliament for his constituency and ask him to arrange interviews on TV and Radio, so he could tell the truth about South Africa.

This was an account, as he saw it with his own eyes and how he participated in the exercise, which disproved everything about black men being trampled upon and having no say in anything in South Africa. According to him, he would tell New Zealanders that the black man he saw, and with whom he had spent some time, was in charge of white detectives, including senior ones, during the course of his being interviewed by the police in South Africa.

Under normal circumstances, this would be excellent news for me, for my colonel, and for South Africa. However, I was a black man who was suppressed and suffered under apartheid with all the others. These were far from normal circumstances!

I would never tell New Zealand and the world that it was not true that black people, even policemen, were discriminated against and oppressed under apartheid rule. I was still not allowed in whites-only facilities. I still lived in a group area which barred me from entering white areas at certain times. Whatever rank I had, a junior constable who was white was still my superior. Indeed, in that whole show, the great ambassador for South Africa was colonel Venter. In his world, that is how things should have been. I wish nobody blamed me for impressing Crowther or giving a wrong impression about the place of the black person in apartheid South Africa. I was only doing the best I could on a platform availed to me at that time.

No one could justifiably fault Crowther either for reaching the conclusions he did, based on what he saw or thought it meant. There was such a complication in how the colonel and Crowther felt – moved by a supposed discovery of non-racialism in South Africa. All of which was the result of meetings with me over a period of one week. The fact of the matter is, though

I liked the colonel as a person, and had every reason that he respected me and liked me for the honest effort I put into my work, I could not avoid or resist an urge. It was an urge to subject the story he had told me about what Crowther had said to deeper analysis. It was an urge to examine what was said about the happiness it gave him and his congratulations for what it would mean to South Africa. I was happy that South Africa was isolated by the world for its oppressive apartheid policies. If ever I were to be called to give evidence on whether economic sanctions against South Africa should have been maintained or withdrawn, my evidence would be in favour of even more strict and sustained sanctions.

I could not understand how the colonel would feel that I would be happy to be known as the black man who saved apartheid. I wondered why he would have thought that what Crowther had said he had observed, was the truth about South Africa, when he (colonel) knew it was not true. What Crowther had seen and heard during the brief moment of our meetings was true as far as his observations were concerned. The whole team could not fault Crowther for his observation. Even the sergeant Chockra was a witness to it, but the colonel and I knew that the discriminatory and apartheid laws were still strongly in place and were a daily reality. In my case, he had gone all the way to ignore petty apartheid practices. However I honoured him for what he did and observed. He treated me like a full grown up and a competent human being. I always thought I had dignity to maintain and protect and the colonel seemed to have observed that and helped me to keep it intact throughout our association.

Colonel Malherbe

Colonel Malherbe was a good man and a good detective; he used to run the marathon from Durban to Pietermaritzburg and the down run from Pietermaritzburg to Durban. He mixed well with all people. Once a month, he would visit Hillcrest Police Station, where I worked, for docket inspection from his office at Durban West District headquarters. In anticipation of his impending visit, black detectives would relax and look forward to a constructive engagement during the inspection.

He was not one of those officers who, when it was their turn to do the docket inspection, black policemen would prefer to leave their bundles of dockets and leave the station. In the eighties, he once found that there was a missing docket that I used to send in for inspection. He noted that he had not seen that docket for three months. I had been hiding it because I had missed submitting it to my branch commander for the regulation twenty-four-hour inspection. That was the problem with dockets. Once it missed an inspection, even if one carried on doing investigations on it, and made entries in the diary to that effect, it became difficult sending it to any inspecting officer, just because of a missing twenty-four-hour inspection. The next time, it would miss the monthly officers' inspection because if he saw it, he would discover that it had not been shown for the twenty-four-hour inspection and subsequently, the ones by the branch commander. In the end, the docket would develop a monster status, which one could only hide by making excuses about it until there were none left.

Colonel Malherbe decided to give me the shock of my life. He called me aside and told me that, on that same day he had come to our police station he had seen the forever missing docket. He told me that I should not try to give any explanations for the docket not being presented for inspection, but he had come to give me some freedom from the stress the matter caused me. He said what he had come to do was to kill the missing docket for me.

While I wondered what that meant, he went on to say that the deal would be that I would bring the docket to him for him to see that I had not killed it myself. If it were to be the case, that I had killed it, the deal would be off.

The worst thing any detective could do with a docket was to destroy it. His offer gave me a bit of relief, because I had never had an idea of destroying the docket in question. I thanked myself for that, but still saw a catch somewhere in what the colonel was proposing. He went on to say, and at the time he seemed amused with himself, "Now sergeant, go and fetch only that docket for me to see and kill for you, so that from today you will be a free and happy man. I know that such a docket could drive you to suicide and I do not want that to happen to you. All your dockets that I have inspected have been very good as you would know by the remarks I have always made on them. Today, I have not come to inspect any of your many dockets, but to see only this one. Also, I will not inspect the docket, but will only ascertain that it is still there, and I will instruct that it be filed. I am doing this because I know that you know what is in the docket, and I trust that you will re-open it should anything positive develop around it. I leave that to you to do because I trust you."

That was too good to be true. I did not know what to think because the air around what he said was charged with honesty. There was no room to doubt him. As such, I went and fetched the docket from where it was hidden and presented it to him. He took it and wrote in the file on the relevant column. Immediately after that he stood up and said, "Get your friends together and go and have yourselves a *braai*."

He deserved more than just a 'thank you' from me. I could give a shoulder-breaking handshake or an Arabic devotee's bow. The gulf between him and me (a white colonel and a black sergeant) at that time would render a hug almost a deadly exercise. I mean I could not thank him enough for that. It appeared that he had left the headquarters only to come and see the ritual we had just gone through, performed, because after that he went to his car and left the station. It appeared that he had not finished with me in terms of the magnetism that kept drawing him to me, to show me what a good human spirit he had.

One Saturday afternoon, I was driving a fairly new Ford police van in Kwa Mashu. The vehicle was only two weeks old. I was involved in a serious accident where the van I was driving became a complete write-off. I was evacuated to the hospital by an ambulance.

As I recovered in hospital, I wrote a poem about the accident. I bemoaned the misfortune I had had; I was also hard on myself for causing irreparable damage to a brand new police van. I foresaw suspension from driving, appearing before a disciplinary committee, or even a demotion. I was also preparing to fight back even before any fight was apparent.

The Colour of the Skunk

Once I was discharged, I went on sick leave for a few weeks. During that time I did not set foot in the police station. I heard that colonel Malherbe had been enquiring about me. I wished that I could find ways of avoiding him.

Then, one day, he asked that I be taken to him. When we met, he looked at me with searching eyes and then said that he was amazed I had looked the way I did. This was because he had been at the scene of the accident where he saw the extent to which the van was damaged. He said that looking at the extend to which the van was damaged, they had concluded that, even if I had survived, I would be wheelchair-bound. He thought it was a miracle to see me walking and talking as I did. On a serious note, he made a short emotional observation to me. He said that he was aware that I was trying to avoid him because I thought that they were very concerned about the new police van I had caused to be written off. He went on to say that, when the police bought vehicles, they bought them by the thousands at a time. However, he told me that I should know that, with all the money they had, they could not buy me. He added that I should know that there was only one of me. He went on to say that they were looking forward to my speedy recovery, and that, on my return to work, there would be another new van waiting for me to use for work.

What he had said to me, and the manner in which he has said it, further confirmed to me that he was a good man. It seemed that individual merit, more than anything else, was his yardstick to measure every man. I honour him for that.

In this, my roll of fame for those whom I have said carried the candle of light in that dark hour in the history of our beloved country, the name of Frank Dutton booms large. Let me also hasten to say those people, as far as I knew, from sergeant Busuidenhoet onwards did not at any time behave and act in the manner they did because they supported the ANC or the Communist Party in any way. They supported me, the South African Police Force and South Africa. Some may have voted for the National Party, architects of the apartheid regime, over the years but the spirit of humanness in them made them to choose in the vastness of all that apartheid could offer to the white people, the happiness that could make them happy if it made everybody happy irrespective of how pigmentation presented them.

Chapter 36
Waving the Red Flag in Front of a Spanish Bull

I will reflect on reasons the police would have used to decide that a 'permanent solution' was necessary to solve the problem they would have foreseen in keeping me around. There was my involvement in the prevention of a cover-up in the matter of the discovery of dead bodies of five black men who had been detained by the police. There was also the fact that, after the Roy Peter Barber case, the Security Branch sent two of their black members to ask me to join them. When I declined, I was told to swear an affidavit explaining my reasons.

In the main, I gave the reasons that it had taken me over twenty years to arrive at the point where they would have thought I would be useful to them. Therefore, because I was then left with less than twenty years before I retired, it would mean that by the time I reached maturity in their department, it would be time for me to retire, which would be a bad result for me.

I also said that because of experience and expertise in my field, I had been provided with a police vehicle, which I took home, and was not obliged to share with others. I foresaw that it would not go down well with my new colleagues in the Security Branch if I were to have a vehicle as a condition for accepting. Owing to the serious nature of the cases I was assigned, I was provided with transportation. It was something I got used to and it was also one of the reasons I was successful as a detective.

I ended by saying that with my network of informers, if I came across something I would regard as relevant to their work, I would not hesitate to alert them. I stressed that I had no other reasons for declining their invitation.

Fortunately, Colonel Venter, with whom I had been involved in the investigation of the Roy Peter Barber case, and who was also a District Head of Detectives in Durban West, said that he would attach his own comments to my affidavit. He did so because he felt that my services were as important where I was as elsewhere.

I was called to the Security Branch Head Quarters and told by a colonel that they did not want someone who would be unhappy working for them because they were a happy family.

No black officer had ever turned down an invitation to join the Security Branch. The subtle, unwritten rule was, 'If you are not with us you are against us.' This was like the proverbial 'waving a red rag in front of a Spanish bull.' For me, the chips were down. It was time for character and principle to manifest.

My bull was neither tame nor lame. I knew that my attitude would not be taken lying down. I had to await their next move with bated breath. I felt that it would be highly unlikely that their analysis of my attitude would produce any outcome in my favour. I just had to keep a stiff neck and move along. I kept remembering the tune *Que Sera, Sera, Whatever will be, will be.*

Chapter 37
Ten O'clock Tea at Police Quarters

Where not every white policeman was a racist, apartheid became difficult to practise. As I have said elsewhere, there was so much to see and learn about the badness and the goodness of people in the journey I had embarked on. It started with the Mullers. The goodness of hearts, I mean up to this stage I had realized that, along a black string of unpalatable events and misfortunes, there would be punctuations of white dots of ease, happiness and wonder – wonder in the sense that the spark of hope and of love and compassion comes from the black and evil coals of extreme hatred and intolerance. It all seems to remind human kind that white will only be clear and recognizable in the mist of blackness.

I had by this time established myself as a detective with a good reputation, especially within the law courts which included state prosecutor lawyers and judges. Whenever I had cases for trial in the courts state prosecutors and judges would send letters of commendation to the district headquarter expressing their satisfaction with the way my cases were investigated and presented in court. Senior officers who inspected my dockets would most of the time write, "Keep up the good work" in my dockets. Some officers would never bother to express any appreciation for any good work done by black detectives. When some of the senior officers came to visit police stations they would have *braai* parties with white detectives at the station after docket inspections. During speeches made by senior officers at the stations where black detectives were in attendance, when reference to black policemen was made they would be referred to as 'you people' as if they were orphans of the police force.

Black detectives had got used to that, yet they were the ones instrumental to the success of every white detective's case, especially those cases where black offenders were involved. White detectives were aware of that but were party to concealment of the fact that their so-called successes rode on the backs of their black counterparts. When it came to the courts, in cases where vital evidence was collected by black policemen working in units where white detectives were in charge, black detectives were said to have been used as interpreters so that they are not used in court evidence as the ones who were instrumental to collecting evidence. This did demoralise black detectives, but here nothing was normal so white policemen got along as if nothing undermined anyone and the blacks who were victims of this kind of undermining just let it go.

All in all, there were senior white detective officers at regional headquarters who were good people by their nature. They were good in their individual ways. The most important feature of a good senior officer was treating all those who served under him equally and without any hints of racism exhibited. Blacks were sensitive to being discriminated against because they were black. They would constantly look carefully for any signs of racism in the behaviour of white policemen especially senior ones, because when senior white detectives were racist it was worse with the junior ones.

I had the honour to serve under an exceptionally humble senior white detective officer from the Durban West District headquarters. He was religious, kind and refined. It happened one day that he was booked to address a meeting with rural leaders amongst who were headmen and (amakhosi) chiefs. He called me into his office and told me what the meeting was about and asked me to help him draft his speech for the for the occasion. He was new in the area and in the province and needed tips here and there in terms of Zulu culture and the prevailing mood of things in the traditional environment of that time and that area. I felt so humbled and honoured by the request that I collected the best of my knowledge on the subject and put together my best 'team' of winning ideas into the draft speech I prepared.

When the officer returned from the meeting, he called me to his office to tell me that the speech was a real winner and that he was given applause at the meeting. I was happy that I played a part in that moment of his happiness and success.

One day I received a call from the colonel asking me to meet with him. When we met, he told me that he had a son who had just started in the detective branch and that he wanted me to mentor him and that he would get him transferred to Hillcrest to work with me. He told me that his son was disciplined and well mannered. I promised to help the boy in the best way I could. Indeed his son came to Hillcrest as his father had indicated. He was exactly as his father had told me. He was very humble and respectful to me, so much so that in the apartheid set up it made me uncomfortable and feared that he might be misunderstood by his white peers and called names so that he would end up being unhappy. When tea time came for white detectives to have tea he would give his tea to me. I would try to avoid an ugly situation by apologizing saying I had just had an orange juice from the tea room next door. Otherwise I enjoyed working with the young man who turned out to be a good listener as well. I learned that he was a champion tennis player and that he played almost professionally and to be selected for championship matches. I do not remember how we parted. I seem to think he got transferred or that he went back to school or something like that.

Some years after that I was asked to go and assist in a case where a member of parliament in the KwaZwulu Government was murdered in KwaMashu. While carrying out that investigation, I found out that the suspects in the case would not cooperate. I wrote a memorandum to the KwaZulu Government requesting authority to arrest and detain them under an act allowing to detain them for three months and over, as it applied to political activists. I could not get a typist to type the memorandum because the team had not been provided with a secretary or type writer.

I happened to call at Durban North District Headquarters and while walking in the yard there I saw the colonel I had long wondered where he had gone. He was very happy and excited to see me. We greeted like long lost brothers. He could not allow me to feel small and made me feel as tall as he was. I feared for him when I thought how his colleagues would perceive him in the mid-eighties tense political atmosphere. It appeared as if the fear was mine alone which did not affect him because he was as relaxed as the old positive and free going type of individual. He invited me into his office and when we got there I told him that I had a memorandum to be typed but was struggling to get a typist. He told me not to worry because his secretary would type it while we talked about old times over a cup of tea. We had been talking for about 30 minutes when the clock struck ten which turned out to be tea time and I saw some officers walk into my friend's office.

It appeared that all the officers had their tea in his office. He also seemed to be liked by the other officers, perhaps the reason they chose to gather together in his office to relax and take tea. I saw that the office was filling up with high ranking officers of the headquarters who were mostly in uniform. I felt very uneasy and told my host that I would take a drive and return in fifteen minutes. He whispered to me saying I should stay put and not be bothered by the other officers.

A white female lieutenant in uniform entered with a large tray plus a large pot of tea and a jug of milk. She placed the tray on the table and left. There was a sudden silence and no one made a move towards the table. There seemed to be a mini crisis in the office.

While it was common practice for white officers, and policemen to drink tea in the presence of black policemen who were accustomed to being made to stand and watch whites drink tea, this was problematic because I was at that time the guest of one of the most high ranking officers in that District headquarters. He had decided not to allow me to go away during the officer's tea period. He could have found me a side office and ordered a black member of the kitchen staff to serve me with tea there. He was aware of the segregationist policy of the country and his duty was to implement them. It was now affecting him directly and was demanding his own personal stand. He had the power and saw the space to express it. I do not know if he contemplated or entertained all these thoughts in his mind but I knew that on that day, 10 o'clock tea time, in his office he lit a little candle of hope for me and gave homework to those present.

While there was unease and silence in the officers facing a tray of tea, the uniformed brigadier who was the most senior in the uniform branch for the district stood up and walked outside. After a little while my host followed him. I was sure there was a quick meeting outside to resolve what seemed to be a crisis. There was still no movement or talk in the office. They came back looking very relieved and with what looked to me like a beautifully arranged psychological plan because when they entered he faked a surprise and said, "Gentlemen, tea is getting cold," and made a point of addressing himself directly at me and said, "Warrant grab a cup and let's have tea." Everybody there took their cups poured their tea and all was well. People started opening up and talking. None spoke to or said anything to me.

That was our apartheid, when a simple thing as having tea with me as a black policeman caused a mini crisis to call for a resolution by a quick meeting of senior officers.

Chapter 38
On the System & its View of Me

Fighting among the leaders of both factions took three months for the Supreme Court to resolve. Some of the leaders were given sentences of life imprisonment.

That was one of the most interesting cases in which I participated in my career as a detective investigator. It gave me valuable and interesting insights into the subject of faction fighting. As well, it gave me an opportunity to examine in depth and research the causes, the manifestations and outcomes of factional fighting. Most importantly, it gave me access to the mind of a faction fighter. I gained valuable experience in dealing with several causes and manifestations of faction fighting; investigative mythology of each towards the achievement of the desired and expected results, which should be mainly the establishment of peace between the factions.

I got involved in that investigation because, although the fight had started in Maphumulo Kraanskop, it spread to Durban and Johannesburg. Two men from a building construction company were killed while sleeping in a shack on the building site in my area of Hillcrest. It turned out that such murders were taking place in the hostels and other places in Durban. Strangers on farms and shack dwellings were also murdered. I asked for a team of detectives to work with me on the cases and was given a chance to select detectives I trusted. I was not disappointed. We had to conduct investigations as far afield as Johannesburg in the hostels where there were concentrations of people from rural areas of Kwa Zulu Natal. I received special commendation by Justice Friedman who presided over one of the cases involving faction fighting. The defence advocate concurred, which was unusual.

On August 2nd 1988, I was invited to give a lecture on faction fighting in a detective course for white members only in divisions of Northern Natal and Eastern Transvaal. This was held at the Benoni Mechanical School from 12:15 to 14:35.

This was a rare honour accorded to a lowly black detective during that time. That kind of gesture by the apartheid police authorities puzzled me.

Back in 1985 I had written a document, titled *Faction fights: Hillcrest, Pinetown, Umbumbulu and Hammersdale* after my involvement in the investigation of faction conflicts in Umbumbulu and surrounding areas where more than 84 people were killed. Somehow, that article found its way to Pretoria Police Headquarters. I was later told that the legal department of the police was using paper in faction fighting symposia at University conferences. One such conference was held at the Ongoye University of Zululand Branch in Umlazi, Durban. I had neither received official recognition in writing nor had there been a comment directed to me about it.

What became a puzzle to me was that I was convinced that I was a marked person and that, somewhere along the corridors of state secrecy, there was or were those who were assigned to watch me. I was not so naïve, nor did I perceive them to be so naïve, that they had no inkling that I did certain things, which in the grand scheme of things under apartheid, I was not supposed to do. I had too much respect for them to under-estimate their intelligence capabilities.

Some of the things that happened, for instance, ordering me to investigate very sensitive matters for them, such as the Kwa Ndebele Government in 1986; and the mandate to bring to court its cabinet minister, against whom I found evidence of corruption, murders and other serious crimes, to be tried and convicted. This had the consequence of shutting down the whole concept of Kwa Ndebele Government as a failed experiment. Moreover, as I wrote elsewhere in this book, I was to report this to nobody, except the General who was in charge of all detectives in the entire South Africa. What else, on earth, did they have to do to convince the world and me that they trusted me?

Next they sent me a letter of commendation for conducting the investigation, despite the fact that their rogue policemen killed the subject of investigation in a car bomb explosion. I had reported to the General that I had completed the task he had given me and was requesting reinforcements to effect what would have been a historic arrest.

In addition to this, police headquarters directed me to go and present a lecture to white detectives only, in an advanced course on faction fighting, which was also a first of its kind in the apartheid police set up. I felt that they had to trust (or is it respect?) one to do that. I wonder what they would have said to those white senior detectives to prepare them to be a receptive, disciplined audience, which they happened to be for me. Surprisingly!

There had been alleged plans to kill me by some rogue members of the Security Branch. The office of the Attorney General was informed and in turn informed the office of the Commissioner of the South Africa Police Force. The matter was also published in the City Press, which reported that a detective was in hiding because of threats to his life. It seemed that, because of this, the would-be assassins decided to withdraw. A member of our unit had met the hit squad members in a police van from Ulundi Kwa Zulu Police Headquarters carrying large bags and when he asked them where they were headed, they told him that they were on a mission to get me removed for good because, unfortunately, I had made it my duty to investigate only Inkatha members. They knew the member was from our unit, but did not know that he worked with me. On hearing this, the member rushed to Pinetown Police Station and reported the matter and subsequently made an affidavit to that effect. Captain Dutton, who was in charge of our unit, offered me refuge in his house for about two weeks, until information filtered through that the operation had been withdrawn.

As a guest of the Duttons, I learnt a lot about friendship that went beyond racial boundaries. He was my superior as far as the work situation was concerned. However, in an ordinary life situations, he remained a true friend and a brotherly colleague.

The respect and care I received in his household indicated to me that he had spoken well of me to all members of his family. In the course of my refuge there, I was treated like a very important person. I saw his wife go through a cookbook as if looking for something special. When we sat down at the dinner table, it was obvious that the meals came from choices of special recipes. I was given a spare bedroom with fresh linen. When I went to the bathroom, there was something new for me to learn. I learned that white people did not use or hang face cloths on the towel rail like we blacks did in the townships or in our bathrooms. It reminded me that even when I used to watch films or new soap adverts I would see the demonstrators in baths or showers running a cake of soap just as it is instead of rubbing with a face cloth. I felt I should not hang my face cloth on the towel rail in the bathroom. Instead, I went to hang it on the washing line outside. I was happy that no one saw the predicament I was in about the face cloths. All in all, the stay at the Duttons was like a holiday spent in a five star hotel for me.

Chapter 39
The Final Curtain

I closed my final chapter as a detective in the South African Police Force with the First Feed Massacre. For me, it was indeed a grand finale to a fine, yet somewhat tempestuous, career. It was a journey characterized by numerous lessons in the art of 'survival in the lion's mouth," as aptly put by Raef Clison in his book *The Invisible Man*. So much depended on whether or not I kept secrets in the midst of bitterness. It was a world where honesty and loyalty had many formidable enemies.

Deceit, cruelty and treachery reigned supreme under the apartheid order. It was sometimes extremely difficult to distinguish between the innocent and the guilty. In the minds of the timid, the brainwashed and the naive evil and destruction could easily, and unashamedly, be disguised as angels on a rescue mission. Good intentions existed side by side with confusion and misconception. In many respects, time and circumstance did not allow for the clarity of minds to sieve through the mayhem that was substituted for the ever-elusive truth.

When I stepped down from the witness box, having given evidence the last time as a detective in a court of law, I felt that I was entitled to be proud of myself. I had ended my career on a very positive note.

My final case was one of the most difficult ones I handled in my entire career as a police officer. There was interference from superiors as high up as Pretoria, from police generals, brigadiers, colonels and captains. Their main goal was to save the black and white policemen charged in the Trust Feed Massacre. We got convictions in the case and the Attorney General of KwaZulu Natal commended us. He actually led the prosecution team at the trial later on.

When I was transferred from Mayville to Hillcrest, my operation area was Hillcrest and the surrounding suburbs. The rural areas were Nyuswa, Ngcolosi, Shongweni and Molweni. They were under Amakhosi (Chiefs) Bhengu, Ngcobo, Mthembu and Shozi. They were vast areas with a large population. Most of the time I used to drive into the rural areas alone. During my time there, I enjoyed the respect and cooperation of Amakhosi, headmen, tribal policemen, most of the law-abiding elders, and the youth who had nothing to do with crime.

I believe that I became popular in all these areas because I was a determined and committed crime-fighter. As a result, I never struggled to get information in order to solve even the most serious cases in those areas. Typically, youths were the ones getting involved in crimes such as assaults, robberies, rapes, murders and breaking into houses. Obviously, these offenders did not line up like fans jostling to be seen bestowing accolades on me, a detective and a policeman. I did not blame them for that, and I surely did not hate them. I hated crime, and everybody knew it. I had an extensive network of informers, even among the criminals themselves. There were also some law-abiding members of the public, living victims of crime, who fought in the forefront with me. That network served me well.

I dealt with pure crime, if there is any purity to be associated with crime; nothing political. The latter was for the Security Branch to handle.

One day, I was surprised to learn, from a political friend, that some of the boys against whom I had cases for housebreaking and robberies, had gone into exile. I was told that they had gone for training so that they could return and kill me. It was reported to me that the criminal suspects alleged that arresting them, the way I did, was a kind of persecution deserving the elimination of the 'persecutor'.

The criminal youth usually broke into white people's houses in the suburbs, which were regarded as areas of low crime rate. The same people found it easier to rob and kill black people, and more black people got murdered than whites, as recorded by every police station. In my experience, I was aware of what could be the boundary between persecution and an honest campaign against crime.

I embarked on a journey of introspection about the allegations of persecution. I still could not find fault in my approach when most of the victims I dealt with were black.

On a more serious note, I had a relative who was a student at Ohlange College in Inanda, just outside Durban. It was during the period of unrest in schools. The student was very worried and came to report that there was a meeting at the college where some senior members of the UDF were present. He added that one of the comrades, who was there, had raised the matter of my campaign against crime. Reportedly, the comrade called my approach to crime fighting persecution, which was the buzzword amongst those who mixed their politics with crime. My relative also said that the discussion in the meeting was around the fact that I had to be eliminated. The issue of how my elimination was going to take place was not discussed or agreed upon. He felt that the details were going to be discussed in the absence of student comrades.

The next morning I reported to my Branch Commander that I had information about a threat to my life. I informed him that it had come from a student. The commanders told me that he would get back to me later on the matter. About ten minutes thereafter, he called me into his office and told me that the young man should report to the station the next morning at eight o'clock.

When the student arrived, the following day, there were two white detectives ready to listen to his story. They asked me to leave them alone with the young man. I did not see that relative again that day nor did I hear from my Branch Commander about him.

About three days later, the young man came and reported to me that the two white detectives came from the Security Branch and asked him to leave Ohlange College. He said they were going to find him a job at a shoe factory in New Germany. I asked him to report to me what they were suggesting he should do for them.

A week later, he arranged a meeting with me. He reported that they had given him a job in the Security Branch, but he would be based in a shoe factory as a security guard. On another day, he informed me that they had arranged for him to join a workers' union and therefore his work was going to involve the unions.

I insisted that I wanted to see what he had written or reported about. It seemed that this was no longer about the threat to my life. He showed me one of the things that he had reported on. I read it and reminded him that some of his reports would cause people's deaths. One day when I met him in town, he reported that he had been warned not to talk to me again; and in fact, not to ever have meetings with me.

I was left with a dilemma, because I could not approach anyone in the political leadership. I would have been putting the student's life in danger. If some comrades learned about him and what he was doing, those leaders could not have helped him either. It would also have been a difficult thing for me to be seen to be involved in such a situation because I was also aware that some comrades were police informers.

Epilogue

This book is about a personal experience account from someone who was not only a front seat spectator but also sometimes a hands-on participant in the goings on pertaining to the political violence that engulfed KwaZulu Natal from the early sixties up to the early nineties. Throughout this period, my participation was in the capacity of a policeman and investigator in some of the major instances of that violence. That is where the analogy of a front seat spectator and hands-on participant comes from. I have written from the position of having been right there in the midst of that violence. I really would not need to engage in a research undertaking or try to accumulate sources of information nor develop a curriculum vitae before a panel to decide how much I qualify to narrate my story of what I heard, saw and did in the apartheid South Africa during its era of unimaginable violence.

To those who want to say there was no third force in the political violence that engulfed KwaZulu Natal and other provinces in South Africa during the eighties and nineties, I am strongly tempted to say that those who maintain this position, irrespective of the overwhelming facts, would be those who benefited from it. Those who the third force masqueraded as helping in the violence lose sight of the fact that resultant funerals took place only in the black townships and rural areas. All powerful, fully resourced and capable security forces could stop the violence at any moment if they so wished. That is if they had no interest in it Believe it or not, this is one subject I have no fear to claim to know. I will give you a few illustrative scenarios for those interested in the truth part of the so-called third force debate.

In 1982, I led an investigation in a faction fighting case between the people of Amangcolosi under Inkosi Bhengu of Kranskop and Amabomvu people under Inkosi Ngubane of Maphumulu. Thirty-two people had been killed in the fight. It all started at a party on the border of Maphumulo and Kranskop District. Only black Zulu men were involved in the faction fight. It spread from Maphumulo and Kranskop to Durban and surrounding areas, in the men's hostels and farm compounds. It also spread to Johannesburg in the men's hostels, mine compounds and townships. We arrested members of both factions and sent them to court where some of them were convicted and got heavy sentences after trials lasting more than three months in the supreme courts of Durban and Pietermaritzburg. After the convictions and sentencing, the honourable Justice Freidman commended me for what he called a good investigation and excellent evidence given in court to which the defence counsel also concurred.

That was black on black violence, without any frills or ambiguities. No other races or policemen or other government agents were involved.

Before that, I had investigated several faction fights in my area, which was then Hillcrest and surrounding rural areas. My team of black investigators managed to subdue the faction fights, which erupted in the rural areas of Nyuswa, Bothas Hill, Ngcolosi and Shongweni Dam. I played an important role in dealing with a major faction fight in Umbumbulu rural area under Inkosi Makhanya and Mkhize where about eighty-four people were killed. Arrests were made and the faction fight was subdued. One of the main leaders of that faction fight was rushed to Ngwavuma District, bordering Mozambique. There had been no suspicion or evidence of any other people involved, except for Zulu black men.

Emerging from the investigation of faction fights in April 1986, I authored a comprehensive document on faction fighting with the heading, *Faction fights: Hillcrest, Pinetown, Umbumbulu and Hammersdale,* which the South African Head Quarters used as an authoritative guide whenever their legal department attended and participated in faction fight symposia in the country.

In July 1988, I was nominated to present a lecture on faction fighting to South African Police Whites only Detective Course from Northern Natal and Southern Transvaal, which was held at Benoni South African Mechanical School.

For starters, blacks did not have the means to finance and sustain the violence during apartheid. The third force did. It had its own interests in the violence. If blacks engaged in the magnitude of violence that reduced their numbers, it favoured the course of the third force, which was very strong and influenced by rogue elements of the National Party Governments security forces. By now, we should be way beyond even debating the issue of whether or not the third force was behind the violence. The National Party Government, by creating homelands with the purpose of driving blacks from the broader, viable and developed economy, knew that the consequences thereof would be divisive, resented and violent. They were prepared for all of that. Security forces to successfully (so they thought) thwart all of this were in their hands. If called upon to be brutal about it, they would not think twice. They had the manpower, the logistics and the money. A divided Black community would be one-step towards achieving the goal of the envisioned National Party separateness of people. If the divisions created between blacks erupted into tribal and political violence it would be at the discretion of the security forces to choose which party or faction to help destroy the other. If there were heavy casualties from both sides the better for them. Remember they would not be in it for the unification and strengthening of blacks. For the weaker and the fewer they were, the better for apartheid.

Some members of the third force paraded before the Truth Commission to confess and plead for forgiveness. How better this fact was and how much others wished it away; it is now a subject of history and graces our archives for posterity.

PICTORIALS

CAREER AND RECOGNITION

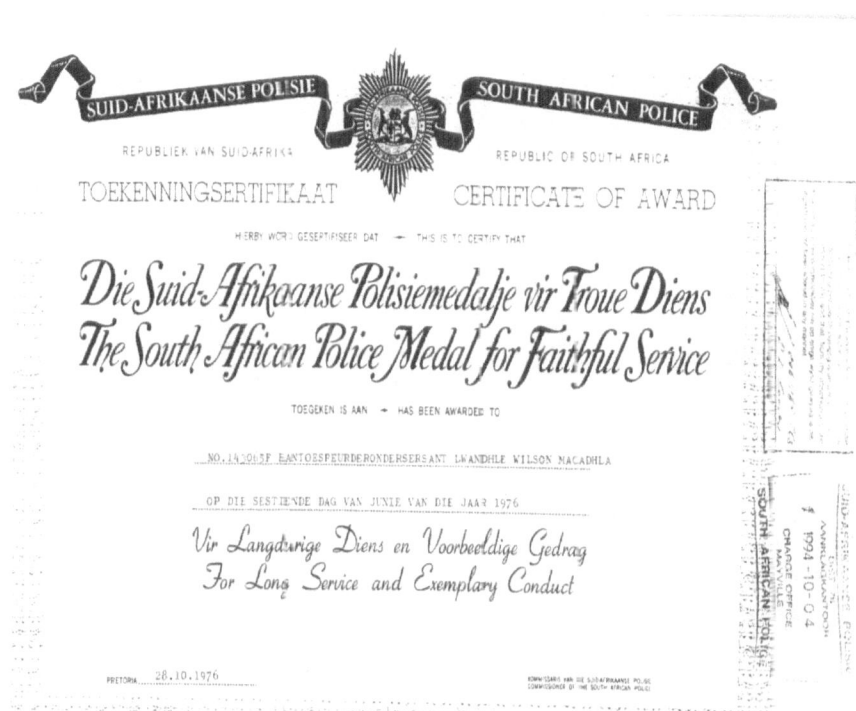

SUID-AFRIKAANSE POLISIE / SOUTH AFRICAN POLICE
REPUBLIEK VAN SUID-AFRIKA / REPUBLIC OF SOUTH AFRICA

TOEKENNINGSERTIFIKAAT / CERTIFICATE OF AWARD

HIERBY WORD GESERTIFISEER DAT — THIS IS TO CERTIFY THAT

Die Suid-Afrikaanse Polisiester vir Troue Diens
The South African Police Star for Faithful Service

TOEGEKEN IS AAN — HAS BEEN AWARDED TO

NO. 8143065F DETECTIVE LANCE-SERGEANT LWANDHLE WILSON MAGADHLA

ON THE FIRST DAY OF MAY OF THE YEAR 1979

Vir 20 jaar Getroue Diens en Voorbeeldige Gedrag
For 20 years Faithful Service and Exemplary Conduct

PRETORIA 1980-10-27

MINISTER VAN POLISIE
MINISTER OF POLICE

SAP 178

BREVET	WARRANT
Deur Sy Edele die Minister van Wet en Orde	By The Honourable the Minister of Law and Order

Aan / To

Kragtens die bepalings van Suid-Afrikaanse Polisieregulasie 13 (2) soos afgekondig by Goewermentskennisgewing 203 van 14 Februarie 1964, stel ek u hiermee aan as 'n Adjudant-offisier van die Suid-Afrikaanse Polisie met ingang van die .... dag van .... 19....

As sodanig moet u derhalwe u pligte nougeset en ywerig nakom in die rang van Adjudant-offisier en persoonlik leiding gee aan al die lede van die Mag onder u toesig en beheer en hulle deeglik oplei en onderrig in al die werksaamhede van die Suid-Afrikaanse Polisie soos van tyd tot tyd voorgeskryf word deur die Polisiewet, Regulasies en Staande Orders asook deur enige ander Wette, Regulasies en Orders wat op die Suid-Afrikaanse Polisie betrekking het.

Verder gebied ek u om al die bevele en opdragte, wat u van tyd tot tyd van enige van u meerderes mag ontvang, stiptelik, ooreenkomstig die Wet, Regulasies, Orders en gebruike van die Mag uit te voer.

Gegee onder my hand te .... op hede die .... dag van .... 19....

By virtue of the provisions of South African Police Regulation 13 (2) published under Government Notice 203, dated 14 February 1964, I do hereby appoint you as Warrant-Officer of the South African Police as from the .... day of .... 19....

You shall therefore conscientiously and diligently discharge your duty as such in the rank of Warrant-Officer and personally guide all the members of the Force under your supervision and control and thoroughly train and instruct them in all the functions of the South African Police as may, from time to time, be prescribed by the Police Act, Regulations and Standing Orders and also by any other Laws, Regulations and Orders applicable to the South African Police.

I further enjoin you to obey promptly, in accordance with the Act, Regulations, Orders and usages of the Force, all instructions and directions you may, from time to time, receive from your superior officers.

Given under my hand at .... day of .... 19....

Minister van Wet en Orde/Minister of Law and Order

Wilson Lwandhle Magadhla

143065-3

Office of the Commissioner
South African Police
Private Bag X94
PRETORIA

1991-11-30

Warrant Officer L W Magadhla
South African Police
PINETOWN

Dear Warrant

On the occasion of your retirement from the South African Police, I would like to thank you most sincerely for the devoted service you have rendered to the State.

Your conduct has proved to be exemplary; an exceptional achievement which shows that you have served the Force loyally and efficiently with an unblemished record.

My very best wishes for the future. May you be spared for many years to enjoy your well-earned pension.

Yours faithfully

LIEUT GEN
f/COMMISSIONER : SOUTH AFRICAN POLICE
P M DU PLESSIS

Brigadier Potgieter
T/WO Strauss
Telephone 031-3604851

0143065-3/6
OFFICE OF THE
REGIONAL COMMISSIONER
REGION "E" (NATAL)
P O BOX 1965
DURBAN
4000

1992-10-08

D/WO L W Magadhla
South African Police
Special Investigation Unit
WARTBURG
3450

Dear Warrant Officer Magadhla,

COMPLIMENTARY REMARKS: ATTORNEY-GENERAL NATAL:
THE STATE VERSUS VAN DEN HEEVER AND OTHER (THE TRUST FEED TRIAL)

Attached hereto a letter dated 24th April 1992, received from the office of the Attorney-General.

Senior management at Regional Head Office have noted with appreciation the contents of the above-mentioned letter.

The initiative and devotion to duty that you and your team showed, is praiseworthy which does credit to yourself and to the image of the Police Force.

Kind regards

f/REGIONAL COMMISSIONER : NATAL
J R S POTGIETER

BRIGADIER S.O.O

ee/6

Office of the CEO
PO Box 3162
Cape Town
8000

10 November 1998

Dear Mr Magadhla

Please accept these copies of the **Truth and Reconciliation Commission's Report** and **Moments of Truth** with our deepest gratitude for your support.

Moments of Truth seeks to capture some of the special events of the TRC. We hope that it will continue to be a historic reminder of the TRC's incredible process.

Your support made a great difference to the work of the TRC.

With sincerest gratitude
   Dr. Biki Minyuku
   Chief Executive Officer

Dr Biki SV Minyuku
CEO

 # National Intelligence Agency

CONFIDENTIAL

NIA/H33/P/04443-78

30 March 1995

MR LW MAGADHLA

PROVINCIAL OFFICE D32/01

Dear Mr Magadhla

APPOINTMENT TO THE POST OF PROVINCIAL REPRESENTATIVE : PIETERMARITZBURG : NATIONAL INTELLIGENCE AGENCY

I have pleasure in informing you that the President has approved your appointment to the post of Provincial Representative with effect from 1 January 1995.

A summary of the more important elements of Conditions of Service (Annexure A) is attached for your information.

Kind regards.

DIRECTOR GENERAL : NATIONAL INTELLIGENCE AGENCY

CONFIDENTIAL

CERTIFICATE OF RECOGNITION

The Truth and Reconciliation Commission gratefully acknowledges you

Wilson Magadhla

for your contribution as a dedicated and committed

Head-Special Investigations

who gave effect to the letter and spirit of our founding Act towards unravelling and recording the painful truth of our past with a vision of building a culture of human rights and reconstructing our country

16 December 2000

Archbishop Desmond Tutu
Chairperson

Martin Coetzee
Chief Executive Officer

LATER CAREER

THE PRESIDENCY
REPUBLIC OF SOUTH AFRICA

Private Bag X1000, Pretoria, 0001, Union Buildings, Government Avenue, PRETORIA
Tel: (012) 300 5200, Fax: (012) 323 8246, Website: www.thepresidency.gov.za

FAX COVER SHEET

DATE: 27 March 2012

TO:	Ms Zimbili Magadla		
Fax :	Tzimbili@yahoo.com		
ENQUIRIES :	Thulani Brenah Mncube		
TEL:	012 308 1925	ROOM NO:	224A East Wing
FAX:	086 683 5433		
E-MAIL:	Brenah@po.gov.za		
NO PAGES:	2(including cover page)		

SUBJECT:	Award of the Order of Baobab:Gold to the late Mr Lwandile Wilson Magadla
MESSAGE:	Dear Madam
	Please find the attached nomination Letter from the Chancery of Orders.

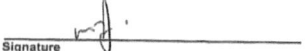
Signature

THE PRESIDENCY
REPUBLIC OF SOUTH AFRICA
Private Bag X1000, Pretoria, 0001

THE CHANCERY
Tel (012)308 1448 Fax (0866835420)

26 March 2012

Ms Zimbili Magadla
59 Horseshoe
Cresent,
Waterfall
3610

Dear Ms Magadla

AWARD OF THE ORDER OF THE BAOBAB: GOLD TO THE LATE MR LWANDILE WILSON MAGADLA

I have the pleasure of informing you that President J.G Zuma has accepted the nomination of the late Mr Lwandile Wilson Magadla for the Order of the Baobab.

The President has therefore decided to honour the late Mr Lwandile Wilson Magadla with the Order of the Baobab: Gold for his excellent investigative skills and pioneering work that led to the uncovering of third forces working for the apartheid security establishment in kwaZulu-Natal that brought the perpetrators of the 1988 Trust Feeds massacre to book.

The Awards Ceremony will be held on the 27th April 2012, at the Presidential Guest House

Travelling expenses to Pretoria shall be borne by this office. You may bring along one personal guest. Please contact Mr Brenah Mncube at tel: (012) 308 1925: cell:0795098717: email: Brenah@po.gov.za regarding travel and accommodation.

You are kindly requested to be at the Presidential Guest House on Thursday 26th April 2012, at 15:00 for a briefing regarding the Awards Ceremony.

Yours Sincerely

R.CASSIUS LUBISI, PhD
CHANCELLOR OF ORDERS

Wilson Lwandhle Magadhla

TRC

Office of the CEO
PO Box 3162
Cape Town
8000

10 November 1998

Dear Mr Magadhla

Please accept these copies of the **Truth and Reconciliation Commission's Report** and **Moments of Truth** with our deepest gratitude for your support.

Moments of Truth seeks to capture some of the special events of the TRC. We hope that it will continue to be a historic reminder of the TRC's incredible process.

Your support made a great difference to the work of the TRC.

With sincerest gratitude

Dr. Biki Minyuku
Chief Executive Officer

Dr Biki SV Minyuku
CEO

The Colour of the Skunk

Wilson Lwandhle Magadhla

It was probably inevitable that doubt, scepticism and even a degree of horror would greet the appointment of a relatively unknown former Durban policeman as chief of special investigations for the Truth and Reconciliation Commission (TRC). But those who know him say simply that Lwandle Magadla is the best person for the post.

FUNERAL

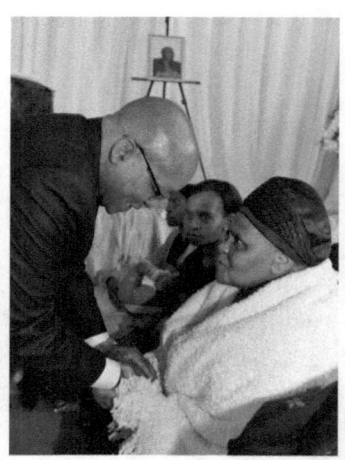
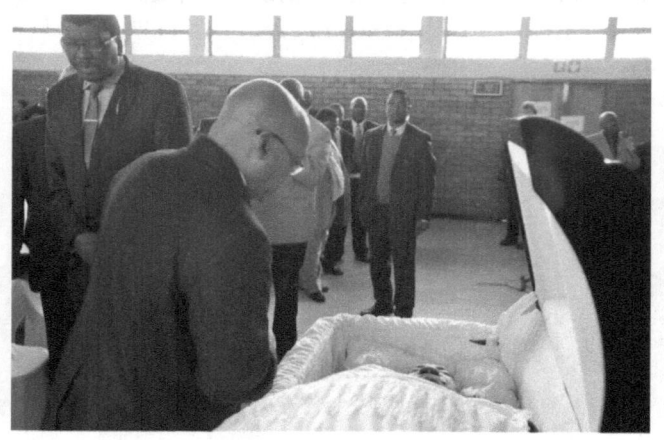

What Others say

As head of intelligence in the African National Congress, I became aware of the outstanding detective work this policeman was performing in the apartheid police force. He was instructed to remain there and let us know what the enemy was planning. Thus he saved the lives of many comrades by warning us when assassinations were being plotted. A diligent, tireless worker who would never rest until the work was done, Magadhla was a raconteur of note – clear and logical. He is indeed an unsung hero of our struggle for liberation who deserves to be honoured by our nation. - *South African President, the Honourable Jacob Zuma at the funeral of the late Magadhla*

www.ingramcontent.com/pod-product-compliance
Lightning Source LLC
Chambersburg PA
CBHW031222230426
43666CB00028BA/1019